Electronic Job Search Revolution

How to Win with the New Technology That's Reshaping Today's Job Market

Second Edition

Joyce Lain Kennedy
Thomas J. Morrow

JOHN WILEY & SONS, INC.

New York • Chichester • Brisbane • Toronto • Singapore

Copyright © 1995 by Joyce Lain Kennedy and Thomas J. Morrow.
Published by John Wiley & Sons, Inc.

All rights reserved. Published simultaneously in Canada.

Library of Congress Cataloging in Publication Data:

Kennedy, Joyce Lain.
    Electronic job search revolution : how to win with the new
technology that's reshaping today's job market / Joyce Lain Kennedy
and Thomas J. Morrow. — 2nd ed.
        p.   cm.
    Includes index.
    ISBN 0-471-11577-0 (cloth : alk. paper). — ISBN 0-471-11576-2
(pbk. alk. paper)
    1. Job hunting—Technological innovations. 2. Job hunting—
Computer network resources. 3. Help-wanted advertising—Databases.
4. Employment services—Automation. 5. Résumés (Employment)—Data
processing. I. Morrow, Thomas J. II. Title.
HF5382.7.K457   1996
650.14—dc20   95-4927

Printed in the United States of America

10 9 8 7 6 5 4 3 2 1

Electronic Job
Search Revolution

For

Nondes Pitman Busby
and
Lowrie Thatcher Busby

My favorite aunt and uncle who kissed my life by making me the favorite niece.

J.L.K.

Maurice E. Stamps

My high school English teacher, football coach, and lifelong mentor, who taught me how to avoid committing homicide with The King's English.

T.J.M.

Foreword

In today's organizations, the term "business as usual" has become obsolete, largely because of the role of technology.

More than ever before, technology has changed almost every facet of business. From telecommunications to robotics, technology has increased productivity and, in many cases, lowered the costs of doing business and the number of people necessary to perform certain functions.

This change hasn't occurred without a price. In recent years, many people have lost their jobs because of the recession and consequent restructuring at every level of almost every organization.

Besides the price paid in real terms by the people who have lost their jobs, the requirements for the remaining workers have increased as organizations have reduced staff while requiring the same work output as before. Organizations must try to get as much as they can out of the remaining employees through more effort, longer hours of work, and new technologies.

Technology has played a critical role in the contraction and restructuring of the work force, but, until recently, it had done little to assist people in their search for employment.

The necessity of a merger between new and evolving technology and human potential has become obvious.

In the job search, this need can be readily seen. The recruiting process was formerly somewhat analogous to a game of darts between novices: hit or miss. Now it is much closer to an art form, as tests and personality profiles give human resource (HR) professionals a better method to match the right persons to the right jobs, before they even meet the applicants.

New recruitment technology allows automatic elimination of candidates whose work experience and particular skill requirements do not fit the profiles for certain jobs, and offers more time to search for the remarkable candidate among a group of excellent candidates. This advantage serves both the human resource professional and the job applicant.

With the introduction of new technology in the workplace, the role of the human resource professional has developed and expanded. Not only must human resource professionals be proficient in the use of new technologies, but they need to know the best way to introduce them to employees, how to improve service, how to make sure that a new technology will not inhibit productivity, and how technology will reduce costs.

Thus, not only the role of technology will shape the work force, but the relationship of technology to the most important aspect of any business—the human component. Human resource professionals, therefore, are charged with merging new technology with human ability.

Past Meets Present

In the past, "personnel" departments benefited least from organizational funding and resources. The job of human resource professionals was to hire workers and to deal with employee problems. Now, the heads of human resource sections are key decision makers and leaders in those same organizations. Input from human resource departments is critical today in the planning and preparation of long- and short-term strategies, and HR knowledge, expertise, and training are invaluable to CEOs as they help map the future of organizations.

The impact of new technology in the workplace does not mean that former elements of the human resource profession are to be discarded. Even with electronic and voice mail systems, the importance of human contact remains extremely important to both customers and employees. Human resource professionals must give this new corporate structure a human face, not only in interviewing, but in explanations of benefits packages, problems in the workplace, safety and health concerns, and termination.

Even as the responsibilities and influence of HR professionals have grown in magnitude and importance, they have not been immune to the overhaul in corporate restructuring. In some cases, human resource departments have been sharply reduced in size, yet not in scope. With fewer people doing more work, technology has had to step in and fill the void. Less time can be spent by human resource professionals to find the right person for the right job. Old ways of resume collection and dissemination by staff are slow, tedious, and expensive.

Fortunately, technology has revolutionized the search for employment itself. A new and ever growing element of the technological age in the workplace can be found in recruitment databases, and there is little doubt that electronic recruitment will become a key component of employment searches—not only for the potential employee, but for employers as well.

More and more companies and their human resource departments are establishing automated applicant tracking systems and resume databases to assist in recruitment. With fewer resources and less time available to them, HR professionals are finding electronic recruitment invaluable.

Technology Meets Tradition

What does this revolution in the search for employment mean for the job seeker? Tried and true techniques of job hunting should not be discarded. Activities such as networking still remain a vital part of the job search. New technology is not foolproof, and letting people know—for instance, in your professional society—that you are searching for employment does and will continue to generate leads and potential results.

The interview still remains a crucial step in employment. However, the initial interviewer may be a computer that tests the prospective employee on his or her knowledge and disposition for solving problems. The results of the computer interview will be available to the second interviewer, a person.

Of all the new technology, resume databases and other forms of electronic searches hold the most in store for people searching for employment. They allow job seekers greater time for research on prospective employers, and opportunities to enter into direct contact with them. Applicants gain the ability to have their resumes read by potentially hundreds of employers for a fraction of the cost and time. The time and money saved can be better used by the job seeker. Thus, although new technology is a useful tool, it does not wipe away traditional methods of the job search—it augments them.

Electronic Job Search Revolution holds vital information about the resources available to merge new technology and the search for employment. This first-of-a-kind book is written in an easy-to-read, understandable style.

Incorporated at every turn are suggestions from human resource specialists to help readers gain a better understanding of how to best use this valuable tool.

Joyce Lain Kennedy and Thomas J. Morrow have a wealth of knowledge and experience in bringing workplace issues and changes to the public, and this outstanding work is no exception. More and more information today is distributed and disseminated through computers and other electronic means, and at this important juncture where technology meets the job search of the 1990s, you will be in a position to benefit through their work.

Technology promises many positive developments for the modern job seeker and the human resource professional. Alone, technology is not enough; coupled with traditional methods of job hunting and recruiting, it can be a pillar of support and an outstanding ally.

MICHAEL R. LOSEY, SPHR, PRESIDENT
SOCIETY FOR HUMAN RESOURCE MANAGEMENT

Alexandria, Virginia

Michael R. Losey is a certified Senior Professional in Human Resources. He is president and chief executive officer of the Society for Human Resource Management, a professional membership organization representing more than 55,000 human resource professionals worldwide.

TRADEMARKS

For readability, in this work vendor names are not set in capital letters, nor are the signs indicating trademarks or service marks used. All known marks are listed below. This list is not necessarily complete. Any use of marked names, whether on this list or not, is editorial and to the benefit of the mark holder. The marks appear below as they are used by the companies holding the marks.

Mark	Mark Holder
Abra Cadabra™	Abra Cadabra Software, Inc.
AbraScan™	Abra Cadabra Software, Inc.
AbraTrak™	Abra Cadabra Software, Inc.
ACCESS®	ACCESS Corporation
AM/2000™	SPECTRUM Human Resource Systems Corporation
America Online℠	America Online, Inc.
APN™	Academic Position Network
Business Dateline® Ondisc	UMI
Business ASAP™ on InfoTrac	Information Access Company
Business & Company ProFile™ on InfoTrac	Information Access Company
Career Link Worldwide™	Career Link Worldwide
Career Doctors BBS™	Career Doctors Bulletin Board Service
Career Navigator™	Drake Beam Morin, Inc.
Career Search™	Career Search
ClassiFACTS®	North American ClassiFACTS®, Inc.
CompuServe®	CompuServe Incorporated
Corporate Jobs Outlook!™	Corporate Jobs Outlook, Inc.
CorpTech®	Corporate Technology Information Services, Inc.
cors™	cors, Inc.
CrossWalk™	CrossWalk™
DescriptionsWrite Now!™	KnowledgePoint

Mark	Mark Holder
DIALOG®	DIALOG Information Services
Dovetail Software™	Dovetail Software™
Dow Jones News/Retrieval®	Dow Jones & Company, Inc.
DowQuest^{SM}	Dow Jones & Company, Inc.
Duns Million Dollar Disc®	Dun & Bradstreet Information Services
EJM^{SM}	Human Resource Management Center, Inc.
Electronic Job Matching^{SM}	Human Resource Management Center, Inc.
General BusinessFile™, Public Edition	Information Access Company
GEnie®	General Electric Network for Information Exchange
HUMAN RESOURCE INFORMATION CENTER™	Computing Management, Inc.
IBM PC®	International Business Machines Corporation
IBM®	International Business Machines Corporation
InfoTrac®	Information Access Company
IntelliView	Pinkerton Security and Investigation Services
Investext®	Thompson Financial Networks, Inc.
Job Bank USA™	Job Bank USA, Inc.
JOBTRAC®	JOBTRAC
JOBTRAK®	JOBTRAK
LEXIS®/NEXIS®	Mead Data Central, Inc.
Macintosh®	Apple Computer, Inc.
Martindale-Hubbell®	Reed Reference Publishing Company
Moody's® Industrial Disc	Moody's Investors Services, Inc.
Moody's® Bank & Finance Disc	Moody's Investors Services, Inc.

Mark	Mark Holder
National Resume Bank™	Professional Association of Resume Writers
Prodigy®	Prodigy Services Company
RESTRAC™	Restrac
Resumix™	Resumix, Inc.
Sharkware™	CogniTech Corporation
SkillSearch™	SkillSearch Corporation
SmartSearch2™	Advanced Personnel Systems
SS2™	Advanced Personnel Systems
TCTN™	The Career Television Network™
The Interviewer®	Global Publishing Corp
TOPJOBS	Dynamic Information System & Exchange, Inc.
Thomas Register of American Manufacturers®	Thomas Publishing Company
University ProNet℠	University ProNet, Inc.
Unix®	AT&T Bell Laboratories
WordPerfect®	WordPerfect Corporation

Acknowledgments

Our thanks to a great many people who have given us their valuable time, support, help, and encouragement, so that we might bring this book to reality. We thank you. And the job hunters of America thank you.

Special Appreciation

> To **Muriel Wallace Turner,** for keeping us on track, on schedule, updated, and uplifted. You're the greatest!

Editorial Support

> **Gayle Leslie Bryant,** The Kennedy Office

Advisers

> **Michael R. Forrest,** National Association of Colleges and Employers
> **Jane Paradiso,** Talisman Technologies
> **Sue Rugge,** The Rugge Group
> **Greg Morgan,** Resumix
> **Peter Weddle,** Job Bank USA
> **Mark Gisleson,** Gisleson Writing Services
> **James M. Lemke,** University of California, Los Angeles
> **Regina Aulisio,** Marketing Professional
> **William O. Warren,** Online Career Center
> **Larry Bouchard,** MedSearch America, Inc.

Publishing

> At John Wiley & Sons: **Mike Hamilton, Mary Daniello.**

> At Publications Development Company: **Maryan Malone, Nancy Marcus Land.**

Contents

Electronic Job
Search Revolution

Introduction

By choosing to read this book, you've decided not to fall asleep at the brave-new-work wheel and miss the turnoff for the future. Job search in the 1990s has a whole new look and, after perusing these pages, you'll be up to date on it.

As we suggested in the first edition, many things change in a period of rapidly advancing technology. Companies open and close, and new developments make obsolete traditional products. We tell you about many of the changes in this revision.

During the past 18 months, we've learned a few things about better ways to explain the technology, too. As one example, the technical name for managing databases of applicant skills is *automated applicant tracking systems*, but another term seems to better communicate the idea: *job computers*. In the revised Chapter 3, we use both as synonyms.

If you're a technological novice, you needn't be apprehensive about what you're about to learn. We tell the complex story in a way that doesn't require knowing "computerese." When we must use technical jargon, we knock it down to the bare minimum and explain what it means in everyday language.

Still not sure you can tell your left hand from your right on a computer keyboard? Think about it this way: You need not understand the inner workings of a clock to tell time. You need not know how to repair a car to drive one. You need not know how to program your VCR to play movies. It's much the same with job search technology: To benefit from this book, you need not understand how a computer works.

When the first edition of this book, and its companion, *Electronic Resume Revolution,* were published in January 1994, few people had heard of the electronic dimension of job search. Since that time, the new electronic ideas and technology have become far more familiar as they continue to spread throughout the American economy.

1

We've received many comments and letters from readers of the first edition:

"Thanks for rocketing me into the 21st century!"

"Where have I been?"

"Relying upon the old ways for secure employment is a comfortable, but dangerously outmoded notion."

"Your books have opened my eyes to what I must do to competently manage my career."

"I enjoyed and benefited from your books . . . which to me were news flashes!"

We appreciate the ocean of kind words and hope this edition proves equally helpful to readers. Here is an overview of what you'll learn chapter-by-chapter:

- **Chapter 1**—an overview of how, in a job search, the computer has become as indispensable as film in a camera.
- **Chapter 2**—how independent database services register people and then permit employer clients to search for candidates who fit the jobs they're trying to fill.
- **Chapter 3**—how jobs are being filled with people whose resumes have been entered into the employer's own database.
- **Chapter 4**—companies and organizations that are operating on-line job databases, including help-wanted advertising.
- **Chapter 5**—the efficiencies of using employer databases to custom-design a list of job prospects. Databases are available on CD-ROM disks, computer disks, and online.
- **Chapter 6**—how the world of computerization has developed to the point where many companies allow computers to take initial applications from job seekers, and, in some cases, administer testing before the hiring process moves to the second level.
- **Chapter 7**—new technological innovations that both you and the human resource specialist can use.

Shall we begin?

1 The New Job Market

Arriving Just in Time: New Tools and Rules for Finding Jobs in a World Where Secure Futures Are Vanishing

This chapter identifies reasons why the job search revolution is racing across the concrete canyons and purple mountains and golden wheatfields of America. It explains how the electronic edge is being used by employers to cut costs, and by job seekers to reach out and take charge of their careers.

Uncertain jobs . . . Variable pay . . . Cliffs of financial anxiety . . . More temporary jobs . . . Longer job searches . . . Lesser known employers . . . Galloping technical obsolescence. . . All these things are happening to job seekers and rising stars alike.

The upside is that wonders may lie ahead. Change certainly does. In this decade that bridges the centuries, a technological revolution is reinventing the ways that people and jobs meet:

- Resumes zap across cities or countries by telephone lines.
- Help-wanted ads flash on home computer screens.
- Vast databases of resumes match people to jobs.
- Resumes are optically scanned, organized, stored, and pulled out in a wink.
- CD-ROMs and video conferencing are used for interviewing.

- Electronic marvels make it easy to customize a blue-ribbon job hunt.

Paper is not obsolete, but it is less important. Resourceful American job hunters are finding something new in the air of America's corporate hiring halls: computer-driven job services.

Before you go into microchip shock, realize you need not have a technical aptitude to "go electronic." You need not even *like* computers to feel the earth move in the emerging upheaval. But the earth is moving: Computerized job services and the electronic recruitment industry are taking over where traditional paper methods leave off.

As technology sparks new ways to look for a job and new ways to find people to hire, the job search revolution has begun.

What forces are spanking new life into a job search revolution at this particular moment in our history? In the ways we look for work, what are the engines driving the biggest employment matchmaking change in a century? Briefly, here's the explanation.

The great job express that rolled through the decades since World War II has run out of gas. As the late Dan Lacey, editor of the newsletter *Workplace Trends,* observed:

"Everything that everyone considers normal about work—long-term steady employment with a full range of company-paid benefits and ever rising wages—is a way of life that came about in America after World War II. It never existed anywhere else."

In the 1980s, American employers, desperate to stay competitive, cut millions of people from their payrolls. The cuts included human resource specialists, who are the gatekeepers for corporate America. The carnage produced a historically significant trend: the steady elimination of millions of jobs that won't be coming back.

An avalanche of company cutbacks introduced a new word in our culture—the dreaded "downsizings." Huge numbers of experienced, qualified workers were thrown into a frenzied competition for jobs. Now, fearful of being overwhelmed with applicants, employers are thinking twice about advertising job openings.

Each time a job opening for a good position hits print, companies are set upon by hoards of job seekers. Because corporate chieftains have thinned the ranks of the human resource departments in the downsizings, they have sometimes left themselves woefully short of staff to respond to hundreds of applications for each job opening. Many companies simply don't have enough people to react in the old-fashioned way—sorting people by hand.

In one instance, a major employer in the Midwest received 10,000 resumes in a one-month period. The human resource staff tried valiantly to cope with skyscrapers of paper by holding "resume parties." At these "parties," a dozen or so people worked in a conference room late into many nights, eating sandwiches and sorting resumes. They saw more of the resumes than they did of their families.

"After finding, say, 172 good candidates for a position, we stopped sorting through—even though we knew the very best candidate may well have been number 173 or 178," says a survivor of the ordeal. "It was exhausting to keep reading resumes after a certain point. And the more resumes we read, the less time we had to interview. It was a Catch-22."

THE NEW ORDER

Moving beyond the technical problem of too many applicants and too few people to screen them, observers generally agree that, philosophically, the United States has become a bottom-line economy. These are the new rules:

- Profit or perish.
- Push for high performance figures for the annual report.
- Get more sales, more revenues.
- Keep the stockholders happy: Keep the company in the black.
- Stay alive: Think *money, money, money!*

In our bottom-line economy, employers are in a take-no-prisoners revolt against hiring costs that have risen like college tuitions. They are constantly on the lookout for ways to trim a budget line and nip an inflated figure.

The trauma and turmoil in the employment arena will continue. Saving on expenses has become a way of life as the nation's businesses fight off global competition, restructure to survive the end of the World War II boom years, and salt away money to buy technologically advanced equipment to stay in business.

The cost per hire for professional and managerial personnel exceeds $5,000. When a private recruitment firm is used, the average cost per hire rockets to more than $35,000.

As employers try to send hiring costs downward, another trend is moving up on the charts: the proliferation of computers in homes, where most job search planning takes place.

In 1994, for the first time, consumers spent as much on PCs as on televisions.

The numbers encourage us to agree with Victor Hugo's often quoted comment: "An invasion of armies can be resisted, but not an idea whose time has come."

Computers are here. People no longer use them as expensive paperweights. People are no longer afraid of them. People who are not the technically elite are seeing computers as one of life's requirements.

Equally important, companies no longer can support the hand-sorting of people that has taken place during the entire 20th century. Manual personnel systems are under intense scrutiny. Their cost-effectiveness is daily questioned by managers for whom the bottom line is sacred.

A marriage of two trends is fueling the job search revolution: unyielding pressure on business to cut costs while dealing with armies of job seekers, and the new wave of user-friendly technology—including the Internet. The result is an explosion of new tools and new rules that is changing forever how you should look for work.

ELECTRONICS: THE THIRD LEG

We live in exciting, if uncertain, times. As the job market revolution happens before our eyes, we strongly urge you to learn to find *knowledge work the knowledge way.* Much as displaced farmers and domestics moved into manual industrial work in the 19th and 20th centuries and learned to find jobs the city way, you must now look in new places and use new tools, or risk being left behind.

Demographers tell us that nearly a half-billion new people will come into the job market during this decade, and that most will come from low-wage nations. If we don't want to work cheaper, we must work smarter to survive as a first-world nation.

Much is at stake as we begin an epochal adventure to install, learn, and apply the new electronic technologies to our job seeking.

At this point, you may be wondering if our urging you to "go electronic" means that advice from traditional job search books and job coaches is obsolete. Not at all. Many verities really are eternal, and we hope you'll heed the abiding truths shared by authors and counselors you admire.

Here's how we see what's happening:

1. "Traditional" job search is the first leg of the process; it includes recruitment ads, third-party employment services, direct application and all the other avenues to employment we've come to expect.

2. "Networking"—meaning the cultivation of large numbers of one-to-one contacts—is the second leg; networking became a buzzword in the 1970s and continues today.

3. "Electronics" is the third leg which has been added to the job search process. It is a mighty new technology to link jobs and people.

What we recommend is that you add a new layer of contemporary information to the knowledge you already have about effective ways to job hunt.

A childhood couplet makes the point vividly:

> Make new friends and keep the old,
> One is silver, the other gold.

The New Job Search Rulebook

You can't count on getting today's jobs with yesterday's search techniques.

Become aware of the digital age as it affects job search.

Anyone who is thinking about the future will have to self-market around the clock.

Educate yourself about being visible in databases 24 hours a day, 7 days a week.

During this time of technology transition, plan on doing a two-tier job search: one for humans, one for computers.

Learn how computers differ from humans in how they read resumes and screen applicants.

You'll create you own job security by developing computer search skills.

From picking through employer databases to online searching, computers have become a friendly way to find jobs.

Never assume the way you've always job hunted is a sure thing.

Consider job search a matter of continuing education requiring lifelong attention.

2 Resume Database Services

Robot Recruiters That Can Do Wonders for Your Career—Or Then Again, Your Name May Never Come Up

This chapter focuses on external, third-party resume database services—independent firms, organizations, and government agencies that register people in their databases and then permit employers to draw from the databases when searching for people to hire.

For job seekers, the lure of resume databases is seductive. If you'd like to have an agent working for you 24 hours a day, 7 days a week, matching—in minutes or even in seconds—your qualifications with open job requisitions, you may get your wish.

The agents that make this magic in blanketing the job market with your qualifications are computerized services. They're called electronic resume databases.

Resume database services are favored by white-collar professionals to parade their qualifications before a wide range of employers.

Recent developments—from the debut of resume database services on the Internet (the global network of networks), to the unleashing of government-sponsored databases that feature jobs for blue- as well as for white-collar people are changing the face of the recruitment database industry.

Electronic resume database services are springing up across the nation as increasing numbers of people discover and use this innovative and relatively inexpensive job recruitment channel.

Database users fall in three main groups:

1. Individuals who hope to find employment quickly by listing their resumes in databases.

2. Individuals who do not necessarily hope to find employment quickly by listing their resumes in databases, but who understand the vital importance of visibility in career management. They're "on display" when employers go shopping for personnel.

3. Employers who search databases to find people to fill open positions. Client employers can use these computerized recruiters with the ease of a few strokes on a computer keyboard or a telephone call any hour of the day and night. The search can be launched from virtually any point on the globe.

One of the things people like about resume databases is that no gate-keeping secretaries are on duty to keep you from recruiters you hope to attract. It's just you and the recruiters—whether human resource screeners or hiring managers.

The premise of the databases is similar, but specifics of operation vary. Most commercial firms and some organizations charge job seekers a fee. Databases sponsored by the government, and some commercial firms and organizations are free to job seekers. (If a fee is due, it is paid by the employer.)

One of the chief trends to emerge in the past couple of years is that great numbers of professional organizations are including a listing in a resume database as a benefit of membership.

When a fee is charged to job seekers, it generally ranges under $100 for a year's listing. Before you sign up, make sure you understand who pays, how much, and for how long.

Even the way the employers cruise through the resume database varies by service. Generally, employers have not been allowed to root around for themselves—the issue is confidentiality. For those services that allow employers direct inspection of the database, the identity of the individuals usually is "cloaked" with coded numbers.

Another common feature offered by commercial resume database services is the option to the job seeker to block one or more specific employers from seeing that person's resume. Still, the entire issue of confidentiality—keeping your resume from landing on your boss's desk—is murky because so many resume databases formerly handled by postal mail, fax, and CD-ROM disc are now available online by computer. (Punch keys or click a mouse on a computer and the resume database pops to the computer's screen.) Often a resume database on the Internet is in a public access area. Within the next year or so, the authors expect that nearly all resume databases will be available on the Internet.

MARKETING FULL RESUMES, SKILLS PROFILES—OR BOTH

Most resume databases are registries of people looking for a job, rather than inventories of job openings. But some services are in the business of listing job openings as well as registering individual applicants.

As we said, each resume database service has its own way of doing business. Some databases electronically scan in job seekers' resumes. Others ask the job seeker to provide specific information on a standardized form that will become a skills profile (also called qualifications summary, qualifications brief, and professional profile). Still other systems use a computer to extract data from a resume and reformat it into a skills profile (also called extracted summary).

Some systems handle everything by computer; others still store paper resumes and send them to employers in support of the selected skills profiles that were sorted by computer.

In any variation, the kind of information you are asked to provide includes the type of position sought, your work experience, preferred industry and geographic location, and professional skills. Some systems ask for your salary expectations or ethnicity.

HOW TO DATABASE YOUR RESUME

As an independent job seeker, you can access the resume database services in two basic ways:

1. *Mail, fax, or hand-deliver your resume to a resume database service.* A summary may be keyboarded into the database by an employee, or a summary and the entire resume may be inserted electronically using a scanner and OCR (optical character recognition) software. (Caution: Faxes or even some dot-matrix-printed materials often don't scan very well. People don't always read them too well, either.)

2. *Use a modem-equipped computer to transmit your resume.* For those not yet literate in computerese, a modem is an inexpensive device that permits information to be transferred from one computer to another via telephone lines or radio waves. A fax/modem is ideal for moving resumes electronically. It works like a fax machine but places information, not a paper message, into the receiving computer.

When you are asked to e-mail your resume directly into a database, the resume service will give you very detailed instructions on how to do it. Again, each service has its own requirements.

As mentioned earlier, some services ask for a paper resume, and others require you to fill in the blanks of a skills profile form. Some request both formats. You may feel that one or the other best showcases your qualifications.

Concepts are another matter; for simplicity in talking about marketing yourself in ways that may be unfamiliar, *we refer to both the paper resume and the standardized profile form as "resumes."*

WHAT RESUME DATABASE SERVICES OFFER YOU

What are the benefits of using electronic clearinghouses that can match job seekers with job openings at the touch of a computer key? We group them into the following main categories.

Access

Have you had this experience? You mail your resume to hordes of employers. You're sure that they *must* have need for the kind of work you can do superbly. And you never hear back or, if you do get a response, it's a form letter rejection ("Thank you for your interest in our company, but . . . ").

Your target companies may be drowning in resumes. They just can't get around to seriously looking at yours. It isn't unusual for big corporations to receive hundreds of thousands of unsolicited resumes each year. Even midsize companies often are submerged in a torrent of thousands of resumes, and smaller firms may be under water with hundreds of them.

When you have what an employer wants, using an electronic clearinghouse makes it more likely that your resume will "rise to the top of the stack" and be noticed. You can get immediate, comprehensive exposure.

Computerized resumes can be accessed and sorted in a number of ways. In a database of 1 million resumes, sorting by occupation, specialty skills, and location preference used to take up to 20 minutes or more to complete; now it takes only seconds.

As one database operator comments, "If a company wants to hire a violinist who speaks Portuguese and wishes to work in Minneapolis, we can locate that person—if he or she exists—in five seconds."

Wider Access

Perhaps the biggest advantage of going online with your resume is sheer numbers. You have the opportunity of putting your qualifications before an enormous number of organizations anywhere in the world—many more than you may be able to place on your own.

Speed

Electronic resume databases can be accessed by client companies quickly. Your background and qualifications become instantly available to employment recruiters.

Cost

Preparing and reproducing quality resumes can quickly eat up hundreds of dollars in reproduction expenses, supplies, and postage. Listing your resume in a database is relatively inexpensive—less than $100 in most cases. It may even be free, depending on the service you select. The free database listings are supported by large organizations that use the services to recruit new hires.

Confidentiality

Your only guarantee of confidentiality is the word of the database service that your present employer—or any other party you specify—will not see your resume. Has the system ever broken down, revealing a job seeker's name to his or her own boss? Yes, one service owner candidly admits. But it was a fluke, he insists, happening only once in three years of operation.

Having issued this warning, we can give you happier news: In the vast majority of cases, it's highly unlikely that your cover will be blown.

Most services do not sell their names for use as mailing lists. Nevertheless, it's prudent to ask. Never assume anything.

Career Management

Database insertions permit currently employed individuals to gain wide exposure to many employers because, in effect, applications can be made after normal working hours. Being listed in one or more appropriate databases is good career insurance. It can become a permanent career-enhancement tool, identifying professional, managerial, and executive opportunities throughout one's career. As part of a positive approach to career management, being database proactive is like being on the right corner at the right time when the right bus comes along.

Who can find out about you—that is, *who knows you*—is just as important to career success as *whom you know*.

An example of the importance of visibility is Tim Harrel (not his real name), a software engineer in Colorado. Harrel was in a commercial resume database for a year and received only two taps on the shoulder. One was of no interest but the second was enticing enough to lure him to Boston. "I would never have known about my excellent current position if they hadn't spotted me in that database," he says.

Fairness

In theory, resume databases allow job seekers to be judged solely on qualifications such as experience, education, and skills.

A recruiter, for example, can tell the system to locate only those candidates who have a specific number of years on a particular type of job, who have worked for specific companies, who have graduated from specific universities, who have particular job skills, and who know specified programming languages.

In the normal course of events, the computer will not weed out female from male candidates or discriminate against applicants from diverse backgrounds or those with disabilities. Reality suggests it probably is too soon to know exactly how the claimed advantage of fairness will materialize.

WHAT RESUME DATABASE SERVICES DO NOT OFFER YOU

Although the rules of job shopping are changing, some things remain beyond the electronic reach. A resume database service usually does *not* offer you the following features.

Personal Representation

As a rule, resume database firms find people for jobs, not jobs for people. Most services are not designed to act as private employment agents.

We hasten to add that there are exceptions, and that there will be more as the industry matures.

Chance to Relax

Just because a resume database theoretically can produce results quickly doesn't mean you can kick back and ignore traditional ways to job hunt. Don't forget about networking, direct application, recruitment ads, and employment services.

If you really want to find a good job, work at your job hunt 40 to 80 hours a week and cover all the bases. This effort, added to your new electronic job search savvy, will put you way ahead of 99 percent of your competitors.

LOSERS AND WINNERS

Unfortunately, job seekers who need employment right this minute may not get offers on that schedule because this method does not tap into the "hidden job market"—unadvertised jobs, in the classic use of the term.

Employers may not even know they need to fill some of these jobs; if they do realize it, they haven't gotten around to the task.

In a computerized job search, you can't persuade employers to create a job or to fill an opening now instead of later. If an employer does not list a job vacancy or search for a candidate to fill it, the match won't be made.

Another aspect of electronic recruitment somewhat modifies that statement. In an employment market where there are many more applicants than jobs, a number of employers are beginning to use resume databases as their initial recruiting effort, to see whether they can fill vacant jobs without the expense of advertising or hiring employment services. By being in a database, you may be able to connect with certain jobs before they are widely advertised. You'll be competing for positions that most people won't even know are available.

Job seekers who stand to gain the most from insertion in computer resume databases are those who have mainstream definable education and skills—particularly technical skills—that can be measured in some way.

As one database specialist explains, "It's a lot easier to match people with 'hard' skills than people with 'soft' skills, but we do receive search orders for personnel with soft competencies, such as cultural diversity management."

Individuals who are occupationally popular in resume databanks include those in such professions as engineering, computer science, chemistry, physics, mathematics, finance, management, accounting, marketing, and human resources.

By contrast, liberal arts graduates who have failed to establish specific occupational expertise may languish in electronic limbo. Others for whom the telephone may rarely ring are those in highly specialized areas, such as fashion design, audiology, and the visual arts. As one service operator concedes, "Your name may never come up."

Job seekers with gaps in their records may avoid being penalized. Computers search for functions, performance qualifications, and total years of experience rather than for chronology. Even so, employers prefer their candidates to have a history of consistently upward movement; when a human recruiter analyzes a resume and finds unexplained voids of time, the resume customarily has been tossed.

The aversion employers have always shown to gaps in resumes may be softening as effect of the deep recession of the late 1980s and the early 1990s.

Line managers—particularly senior line managers—are most forgiving of breaks in the work history. They're often worried about their own job security and can identify with the problem of unaccounted-for months or years. Human resource staffers are somewhat understanding as well. But executive search consultants, who are retained to go after the cream of the crop on another company's payroll, may see a gap as disqualifying.

Job seekers who have obsolete skills are not good candidates for job matching through resume database services. Typists rarely are called for these days. Bookkeepers, switchboard operators, statistical clerks and bank tellers are among others whose occupations are melting down.

Why are job hunters who are out of the mainstream unlikely to turn up on a computer match? Computers can be persuaded to match criterion-for-criterion; they search for "keywords" or "descriptors."

As an example of why it's risky to rely on computer matching when you don't fit today's high-demand criteria, assume a search is begun for a medical technologist.

The keywords may include such terms as *complex laboratory tests, BS degree, cellular morphology, calorimeter,* and *spectrophotometer.*

If you are a medical technologist but have been out of the market so long that your credentials match only the first three keywords and not the last two, you probably won't wind up on any resume database's short list of candidates.

By contrast, using person-to-person networking techniques to search for a job, you may be able to persuade an employer that you're so intrinsically good it's well worth the effort to bring you aboard and "upskill" you with on-job training.

One executive search specialist speculates, "Electronic resumes are okay when looking for limited identifiable, measurable skills—particularly in a $25,000 to $75,000 range—but they do not reflect a job hunter's strength in ambition, motivation, loyalty, critical thinking, resourcefulness, and other desirable human characteristics. Computer search identifies 'things,' not personal attributes."

Admittedly, such human factors are judgment issues that can be evaluated in interviews. But, by artful statements, it's possible on paper resumes to suggest desirable traits.

A new graduate, for example, can communicate a characteristic of "determined follow-through" by commenting that he or she earned 70 percent of his or her college expenses.

Positive traits can be conveyed in documents processed through resume database systems that make available to employers a paper copy or an electronic image of the original resume. Systems that use standardized formats make it difficult, and sometimes impossible, to convey those traits.

The risk is that the exclusive use of fixed-format data can lead to premature disqualification. In cookie-cutter sameness, only core facts count. The people who have the most requested keywords rise to the top. If the job order calls for three years' experience and you have two, for instance, your name may not be plucked from electronic storage. Keep this point in mind when you are selecting a resume database service.

Electronic resume database services are designed to make it easy for employers to pick out the "most qualified" candidates. If your credentials, including education and experience, do not conform to the hiring criteria sought in today's job market, it's chancy to rely on computer matching to find employment.

Although you will layer your new knowledge atop your understanding of conventional methods of job finding, we advise you to assign the highest priority to mastering the high-tech job search strategies described in this book. We further recommend you study our related book, *Electronic Resume Revolution,* which offers new tactics to implement the high-tech strategies.

Electronic recruitment is the direction in which hiring is heading. Even though you've never looked for a job this way before, why not toss your hat into the resume database ring and see what happens? Especially if the listing is free.

When your credentials are in demand, a resume database service can open infinitely more doors than you may be able to open on your own.

TYPES OF RESUME DATABASE SERVICES

Although some firms focus exclusively on technical personnel, generally speaking, resume database services are not yet as specialized as employment agencies, executive recruiters, and other types of employment services.

A few firms open their doors only to recent college graduates. Others include only graduates of specific participating colleges and universities. Still others deal only with specific minority or ethnic populations.

Most are interested solely in experienced individuals. And, rather than concentrating on a narrow pool of talent, most services cover the employment spectrum A to Z.

As the industry grows, expect greater specialization because companies often use specialized resources when they attempt to fill a position. If you have skills in a specific or technical field, such as marketing or math or engineering, be certain you're listed in the resume databases most likely to act as a magnet for employers seeking people with your qualifications.

WHO SHOULD PAY FOR SHOWCASING YOU?

Because it's uncertain whether your name will ever come up in a job requisition search, *we think the only people who should pay for getting their names included in a resume database are employed people who have experience and skills to offer and who view the highly visible listing as a career management tool.*

One operator who charges for resume inclusion takes issue with this advice, making this argument: "Companies in our industry charge a registration fee as a means of assuring that higher quality resumes are submitted. In the absence of a fee, an electronic service can be perceived as a casual 'bulletin board' to which any information might be submitted."

"Charging a fee is one way to eliminate casual job seekers while enabling us to provide prospective employers with uniformly high-quality information about individuals."

In deciding whether to pay for inclusion in a resume database, a key decision factor is the attractiveness of the database to employers. What will make them want to browse through it—size, selectivity of quality candidates, cost of access, geographic area covered?

In some cases, the larger the database, the more attractive it is to employers. Most resume databases incorporate "search engines" permitting employers seeking specific types of workers to retrieve them quickly, rather than being forced to prowl through the entire database.

Selectivity is another issue. If the service is filled with highly qualified individuals not easily available in other collections of resumes, the database will be attractive. In this sense, a resume database of seasoned tax experts, for example, holds the same kind of appeal for employers as an executive recruiting firm that specializes in seasoned tax experts.

Cost to the employer is another factor. Some employers will search any database that's free or low cost, while others assume you get what you pay for, that no or nominal cost equates with a little-value database of pedestrian job seekers.

Relocation costs drive preferences for many employers today. A database that contains a heavy component of resumes from a specific area, say, Southern California, is very attractive to Southern California employers. Recent studies by *The Fordyce Letter,* a leading newsletter for employment specialists, reports that the vast majority (74 percent) of employers will accept a less qualified candidate who is local, rather than a more qualified candidate where relocation is required.

We suggest that you insert your resume in any free resume database—providing that cloaking and confidentiality factors are present. When you have to pay, exercise the same care you would take when making any investment.

ARE RESUME DATABASES WORTH THE EFFORT?

In reviewing the resume database industry for the past couple of years, we have seen scores of examples of people finding jobs, but no hard data exists. Why? A resume database firm's role in a job search usually ends once the job seeker's information is passed on to employers. Unless a special effort is made to survey companies and candidates to learn whether hiring has taken place, database firms have no way to accurately track their success rates.

College career development professionals who communicate with each other on the Internet say they've seen little evidence that the resume database approach works well for new college graduates. That may change with a massive new effort being made through *JobWeb,* a service of the National Association of College and Employers (see Chapter 7).

A GENERAL IDEA OF HOW DATABASE SERVICES WORK

Particulars vary among services, but here's an outline of what happens to your resume once it's inserted into a database:

1. The employer's job requisition is entered into the system.
2. The computer searches for "keyword" matches to the requisition. Suppose the employer is seeking a research engineer with an advanced degree in electronics. The company operates a plant in Tijuana, Mexico, so the candidate should be able to speak fluent Spanish. Because, in lean economies, employers resist the high

cost of relocating personnel, the company is particularly interested in candidates who live in San Diego County, California.

The service's representative keyboards in these requirements, entering them via such key abbreviations and words as *MS, PhD, Electronics, Spanish,* and *San Diego.*

The computer searches the database for people whose resumes match the above criteria.

In minutes, perhaps seconds, the number of matches that contains all of the requested criteria will appear on the representative's screen.

In some systems, the matched candidates are reported alphabetically. In most systems, they are ranked against each other. For instance, a company seeking an executive with a background in finance, production, and distribution will first be presented with a slate of candidates who have those skill sets, followed by a descending-order ranking of those who have experience in only two of the target fields.

Weighting is popular in technical fields where a number of abbreviations are identified and sorted. In recruiting a chemical engineer, the candidates who know the most chemical processes required by the employer are at the top of the report; those who know the fewest are at the bottom.

3. Employers receive candidate reports. Some resume database services, in their initial report, provide only electronic capsules, which may not be to job seekers' advantage. Too often, the computer reports make candidates "blur into a blob of mayonnaise" is how one human resource manager describes computer summary reports.

In most cases, you would prefer to have a resume transmitted to employers. It may be a paper version or an electronic image. It may be sent by e-mail (an electronically transmitted message) from computer to computer in the original format from which a summary was drawn.

4. The employer reviews the candidates, maybe as many as ten, and extends an interview invitation to the most promising, often three to five.

Having your resume referred to an employer through an independent resume database will not guarantee you'll be contacted by that employer. But you're certainly ahead of the pack because your qualifications meet the employer's requirements.

A HISTORY OF THE FUTURE

The archives are thin, but computerized storage of resumes appears to have begun in the mid-1960s, when the National Association of Colleges and Employers began operating two computerized job matching services: GRAD (Graduate Resume Accumulation and Distribution), a service for experienced professionals, and GRAD II, a service for college seniors. The systems featured the resumes of alumni and students at some 1,200 colleges and universities and made them available to more than 500 companies.

A recessionary economy in the early 1970s closed the service, but the software was made available to colleges to develop their own systems.

A number of the pioneering resume database companies did not weather economic storms and closed their doors in the 1980s. Dozens have opened and closed since the mid-1980s—in some cases, taking with them job hunters' registration fees. Perhaps they were too far ahead of their time.

There's a reason electronic recruiting is an idea whose time finally has come: We live in a bottom-line economy. The bottom line of the balance sheet has become a metaphor for the conclusion that the only thing that matters is how much wealth is left after doing business.

Cost-conscious employers are beginning to balk at the cost of print advertising. Three insertions of a 2-column, 3-inch display ad in the pages of a metropolitan newspaper can cost in excess of $4,500; for the same insertions in a national business daily, the cost tops $8,400.

Employers are beginning to avoid fees of recruitment agencies and services. Third-party fees often run into many thousands of dollars for a single hire. Fees vary widely, often ranging from as low as 1 percent to as high as 34 percent of the base salary.

Even so, problems exist in the recruitment database industry. Operators must constantly promote to fill their databases with enough resumes to make them interesting for employers.

Employers are highly specific in their requirements for managers and seasoned professionals, which makes matchmaking a challenge. "And, to compound the difficulty of obtaining high-volume, quality matches for mid-career candidates, employers insist on certain personal qualities and intangible skills that cannot be captured on paper and therefore cannot be identified in a database search," says an East Coast resume database service owner who has wrestled with the problem.

Remember, the dynamics of any new industry are fluid. The electronic database industry is literally inventing itself as you read these words. Companies enter and exit on a continuing basis.

Opening an electronic resume database service is fairly easy because it is not as capital-intensive as some other attractive business ventures and it does not require licensure. "It only takes a PC for someone to open a resume database firm," says Pete Weddle of Job Bank USA in McLean, Virginia.

As the industry matures, some companies will fail or merge not unlike the video store industry, which was once crowded with mom-and-pop stores and is now dominated by large chains. One observer expects that either one (or a few) major resume database service will emerge, or lots of little firms will serve niche markets.

The electronic recruitment industry is unfamiliar to most of us. For your clearer understanding, we've included in this chapter a sampling of independent resume databases: their size, type, and sources of resumes; how they work; who pays the costs; the various types of client employers; and how to enter your resume, how to revise it, and how long it is retained.

We have not attempted to profile all the new resume database services springing up.

Ongoing visibility in a database is one more good reason why savvy career self-managers belong to professional associations.

The profiles we've chosen will help you to compare services at a glance and decide which are best for you.

If, by the time you read this book, any of the services listed have become extinct, it still will be helpful to understand how they function because similar firms—with refinements based on early experiences of pioneers—probably will have rushed in to replace them.

Whether you decide to try any of the services we discuss in this chapter or a new service you find on your own, we suggest you do the following research:

1. Get answers to these questions:

   Does this service reach the type of employers I want?

   Does this service inventory the types of jobs for which I qualify?

   For what reasons is this service attractive to employers?

   How many searches per month does the service process for client employers?

Does the service maintain statistics (not guesses) on the numbers of referrals I might expect per month?

Is the service willing to offer suggestions on how I might improve my computer-match rate, such as revising my resume or refocusing my search?

If I must pay a fee, does the service provide a bonus period of free enrollment if I do not receive at least two referrals per year?

Is there an additional charge for revising or updating my resume?

Does the service provide employers with a summary of information about me? My original full resume? A standardized profile form? Is it electronically transmitted? Mailed? Faxed?

Does the service provide a list of employers currently using the database? (Beware of extensive lists. Half or more may be companies that haven't requested a search in months or even years. It's best to ask.)

2. Check with your local Better Business Bureau to be sure there are no negative reports. Even when you're in Topeka and the service you're considering is in New York, any Better Business Bureau can tap into its national network and request information on any company anywhere in the nation. The Bureau is into the Computer Age, too.

    Even when your resume is included at no charge, you want to be assured of confidentiality and the proper use of your name.

    In any industry, particularly a new one without established rules and regulations, the potential for rip-offs, scams, or just plain ineptness occurs. We've made every attempt to determine that, as of the time this book went to press, all of the services we've listed are active, legitimate, and doing what they say they'll do. Making an inquiry through a Better Business Bureau costs nothing but your time.

WHEN RESUME DATABASE SERVICES REINVENT THEMSELVES

A number of the independent resume database services noted in the first edition of this book have folded their tents. Others, notably *Access* in Kansas City (telephone 800-362-0681), have seen the databases as an incubator and moved from retail to wholesale status. That is, they are paid by employers to operate as a service bureau to automate the entire recruitment process for Fortune 5000 companies and major consulting firms. *Access* specializes in data processing occupations.

Data processing job seekers will be interested in new *Access* services, ranging from an Internet World Wide Web site that links you to many other job resources, to an Internet-wide sweep that matches your resume against all open job requisitions. (The web address is http://www.accesscorp.com.)

SAMPLING OF INDEPENDENT RESUME DATABASE SERVICES

Here is a roundup of some of the leading services. Before sending your resume or enrollment fee, it's a good idea to call any database you're considering and to confirm that its policies and prices have not changed.

▶   **Career Net Graduate:**   643 W. Crosstown Parkway
Kalamazoo, MI 49008
Telephone (616) 344-3017

Size and Type of Database

Thousands of college student/new graduate job seekers who wish access to 10,000 employers, including many Fortune 500 companies who hire people across the spectrum of career fields.

On the drawing boards at press time: Career Net Advance, a resume database operating much the same for experienced workers as the one for new college graduates.

How the System Works

Job seekers use a Windows-based floppy disk to submit resumes, which are combined by the thousands on CD-ROM discs distributed to employers. Employers can search the CD-ROM discs by keywords.

Who Pays and How Much?

Job seekers pay less than $100 to be entered in the database.

Type of Client Employers

All categories of employers, from megacorporations to nonprofit organization.

How Do You Enter Your Resume?

Purchase the software package, load the Windows-based program onto your computer and follow the instructions. Once you've completed the step-by-step process and saved your resume on the diskette, postal mail it to Career Net.

How Long Is a Resume Retained?

One academic year—about nine months.

How Do You Revise Your Resume?

It's automatically revised two times through "bounceback" cards and redistributed with each revision.

▶   **cors:**   One Pierce Place
         Suite 300 East
         Itasca, IL 60143
         Telephone (800) 323-1352 or (708) 250-8677
         Fax (708) 250-7362

Size and Type of Database

This Chicago-based service boasts more than 1.5 million resumes. When researching the database, cors has the capacity to sort in a myriad of ways, which makes it unlikely that any appropriately qualified individuals are overlooked. Both entry-level and seasoned individuals in all fields are in the database.

   Networking contacts are used to enhance database searches. If the research doesn't reveal an appropriate candidate, cors research analysts contact the nearest matches and keep networking until they identify individuals who are close matches to the job requisition.

How the System Works

1. This service takes assignments from employer clients. Job specifications are a starting point for every networking assignment and database search.
2. Once the resumes have been selected, cors personnel contact each individual job seeker to determine interest in the client's opportunity.
3. Once an individual is hired by a cors client, his or her name and resume are purged from the database.

Who Pays and How Much?

The job seeker pays a $25 processing fee to have a resume entered into the cors database. The employer clients, who reportedly number more than 5,800, pay cors a fee to research and identify qualified professionals.

Type of Client Employers

Clients of cors reportedly consist of organizations in most vertical markets, including manufacturing, financial, insurance, retail, transportation, health care, computer consulting, telecommunications, and service-oriented companies. Clients reportedly range from small businesses to Fortune 500 companies.

How Do You Enter Your Resume?

Call cors toll-free (except in Illinois) and give the representative your name and brief history over the phone. You can then fax or mail your complete resume and a check for $25 to the address given above. Cors will enter your resume and confirm the process via telephone or mail.

How Long Is a Resume Retained?

According to cors, a resume is retained indefinitely. Within the database, cors separates the resumes according to the length of time since the last contact by a cors representative for a position. The resume is placed in an inactive file when an individual cannot be located at a work or home address.

How Do You Revise Your Resume?

Revisions of data are simple. After payment for entry of the original resume ($25), the job seeker receives a designated note number for updating purposes. The individual can submit any changes via telecommunications (telephone or fax) or in writing. All correspondence should be directed to the cors Client Services Department. There is no charge for the updating service.

Other Facts

In what may be a breakthrough service in this industry, cors will conduct a unique job search for the job seeker upon entering his or her resume into the system. For an additional $50 fee, cors will match the resume, with help-wanted ads in 70 leading newspapers, as well as with openings in its client base.

▶ **Electronic Job Matching:**   1915 N. Dale Mabry Highway
Suite 307
Tampa, FL 33607
Telephone (813) 879-4100
Fax (813) 870-1883

Size and Type of Database

Electronic Job Matching (a service of Human Resource Management Center, Inc.) says it is a computerized database/decision support system that documents job candidates' credentials and preferences much more comprehensively than does a resume alone. Employers can dial directly into the computer system to do their own searches.

The service uses both a resume supplied by the individual and a supplemental sheet listing job-specific skills, proficiencies, and other information on abilities that the candidate may possess but did not include in his or her resume. Electronic Job Matching (EJM) reports that this extra effort helps make sure an individual possessing the background specified by an employer will not be overlooked simply because a keyword or phrase was left out of the resume.

EJM is composed of many different online services and databases tailored to serve the diverse needs and interests of various job seekers and employers. Collectively, many thousands of job applicants are represented in the system. Individual smaller databases permit highly focused representation for each job applicant.

How the System Works

1. EJM creates an electronic portfolio for each job seeker. The portfolio represents the person's career objective and talents in far more detail than would a resume alone.

2. A job seeker's portfolio is stored on EJM's computer and is available to every employer with a computer.

   When confidentiality is important, the job seeker's identity is kept private, by coding, until a legitimate employer interest is established. Names, addresses, and the names of current and previous employers are withheld until a prospective employer's interest is confirmed. As a further safeguard, a job seeker may block any specific employer from ever viewing his or her profile, no matter how ideal the match.

3. Upon receiving search orders, EJM guides employers through the process of determining their search criteria. Because employers are given direct access to appropriate job seeker portfolios, they make their own slate of selections. Note one important point: Even though employers

have direct access to job seekers, only those portfolios that match—and are not otherwise blocked by the job seeker's request—are presented for employer review. No employer has indiscriminate access to all job candidates.

Employers, when accessing EJM, are asked for such information as job-specific skills with desired proficiency level, industry background wanted, maximum salary to be offered, minimum years of education, work experience required, relocation factors.

Because job seekers are asked for similar information to supplement their resumes, the accuracy of the match can be much greater and the likelihood of overlooking an appropriate candidate is minimized.

Who Pays and How Much?

The EJM service is free to individual job seekers. Employers pay a fee based on time connected to the system and, in some cases, the number of profiles selected. The average employer's search takes about five minutes.

Type of Client Employers

Each database services specific job seeker interests and categories of employers and industries. Employers include both small and large entities. This is a brief sampling of industries served:

Banking

Business services

Data processing

High technology

Manufacturing

Medicine

Publishing

Service industries

How Do You Enter Your Resume?

Mail your resume, and an indication of the kinds of positions for which you'd like to be considered, to the address given above.

An EJM job seeker packet with supplemental forms will be returned to you for completion (takes about 20 minutes). Within 24 hours of receipt of the forms, your electronic portfolio will be available to employers throughout your local community and nationwide, as you desire.

To access the system, employers first must contact EJM (at one of the telephone numbers listed above) to obtain a unique set of passwords and instructions on how to use the system (at no charge).

How Long Is a Resume Retained?

Electronic portfolios, which include the resumes, are kept active and on-line until job seekers are hired, or for a period of four months. Your listing may be extended for additional four-month periods free of charge, but you must contact EJM and request the extension(s).

How Do You Revise Your Resume?

Your resume, as well as any of the additional information gathered about your credentials, can be updated at any time simply by notifying EJM by mail of the changes.

Other Facts

EJM has been chosen as one of the top 20 new human resources services in the nation by a human resource trade journal. EJM also is utilized in the Educational Testing Services' WORKLINK national school-to-work transition service, and in the Urban Leadership Career Network sponsored by *Urban Business* magazine.

▶ **Gonyea & Associates, Inc.:**   3543 Enterprise Road East
Safety Harbor, FL 34695
Telephone (813) 725-9600

Size and Type of Database

Help Wanted-USA is a database loaded with help-wanted ads from more than 50 U.S. cities. All positions are professional in nature, which are updated weekly. This commercial service includes up to 10,000 help wanted ads.

How the System Works

The Help Wanted-USA database is available for searching on America Online subscribers as well as individuals who have access to the Internet. If you prefer, you can have a search of the Help Wanted-USA database conducted for you on a weekly basis with a list of want ads matching your specific goals sent to you. You also may have the weekly database mailed to you on a diskette, which allows you to do your own search on your home computer.

Who Pays and How Much?

For online users, there is no cost for individual job seekers other than the AOL or Internet access fee. There is a $39.95 fee for a six-week subscription for those wanting the job search done for them on a weekly basis, or the diskette sent to them.

▶ **HispanData:**   360 S. Hope Avenue
                     Suite 300-C
                     Santa Barbara, CA 93105
                     Telephone (805) 682-5843
                     Fax (805) 687-4546

Size and Type of Database

More than 15,000 resumes of Hispanic college-educated individuals are in HispanData at any given time. The service offers a spectrum of professional and managerial fields, including:

Accounting

Computer science

Engineering

Finance management

Human Resources

Management

Marketing

Mathmetics

Physics

Sales

Positions are mid-level, requiring three to five years' experience, or entry level for new college graduates. A 3.0 grade point average is required for new graduates but not for experienced job seekers.

How the System Works

1. Employers provide HispanData with job specifications for each position.
2. HispanData personnel search the resume database to identify qualified candidates.
3. HispanData personnel call each potential candidate to prescreen the job fit as well as to verify availability and interest in the opening.

4. HispanData provides employers with a paper resume for each qualified candidate. The salary issue varies: A pay range for the position may or may not be revealed, or an applicant's salary requirements may or may not be requested.

5. Employers contact potential candidates to arrange for interviews.

Who Pays and How Much?

Job seekers pay a one-time $25 listing fee to the service. Employers purchase annual contracts from HispanData.

Type of Client Employers

Fortune 1000 corporations, nonprofit organizations, and government agencies that desire to achieve diversity or meet affirmative action goals subscribe to HispanData.

How Do You Enter Your Resume?

Verify that there are no changes in requirements by calling HispanData. Along with a $25 check, send a single copy of your resume to the address given above.

How Long Is a Resume Retained?

Each resume remains in the database for life; HispanData sends update forms every six months.

How Do You Revise Your Resume?

Contact HispanData by mail, sending a revised resume, plus $10 update fee.

Other Facts

HispanData is reportedly the leading database of Hispanic professionals, who generally are bilingual.

▶ **International Career Information:**   111 Pavonia Ave., East
                                          Jersey City, NJ 07310
                                          Telephone (201) 216-3147
                                          Fax (201) 216-3117

Size and Type of Database

International Career Information, Inc., is a Jersey City, N.J.-based electronic resume database containing more than 25,000 degree-seeking bilingual

Asian college students who are studying in the United States. The service is a subsidiary of database company in Japan, Recruit Co.

How the System Works

Students enter their resumes with ICI, who in turn, sells its database information to companies who have job opportunities, or who want to sell goods and services to these students.

ICI also can provide a list of students gleaned from the database to fit the job specifications and requirements laid down by a client company.

Who Pays and How Much?

Employers pay.

Type of Client Employers

Multinational companies, particularly those with offices in Asia.

How Do You Enter Your Resume?

Fax or postal mail; e-mail was under development at press time.

How Long Is a Resume Retained?

One year.

How Do You Revise Your Resume?

Send in a new resume with a cover letter prominently marked "Revision."

▶ **Job Bank USA:**   1420 Spring Hill Road
Suite 480
McLean, VA 22102
Telephone (800) 296-1USA
Fax (703) 847-1494

Size and Type of Database

Job Bank USA says it has inventories of more than 30,000 + resumes at any one time. It is a nationwide, comprehensive, all-purpose recruiting resource filled with resumes of individuals in all occupations, at all experience levels, across all industries and service sectors.

Sample job titles are:

Attorney
Benefits administrator

Buyer/merchandiser

Chief executive officer

Chief financial officer

Design engineer

Director of nursing

Executive vice president

Industrial hygienist

Logistics coordinator

Marketing manager

Manufacturing manager

Mortgage broker

Office manager

Paralegal

Programmer

Restaurant manager

Sales representative

Secretary

Tax assistant

Vice president

Wellness manager

How the System Works

1. Individuals complete a short enrollment form and attach their resume or employment record to enter their qualifications in the Job Bank USA database. Individuals are contacted within ten days to confirm enrollment; they are given a toll-free telephone number for updating their records.

2. Employers purchase annual subscriptions for a specified number of job searches. For each search, employers call a telephone number and provide job specifications to a professional recruiter on the Job Bank USA staff. The recruiter searches the database to identify qualified candidates.

3. Job Bank USA recruiters call each qualified candidate to verify qualifications and availability, as well as interest in the job opening. Enrollment records of the qualified candidates are updated and augmented to reflect new information about the candidates that is relevant to the open position.

4. Job Bank USA does not refer an individual's record to a prospective employer without the individual's permission. The prepermission policy is designed to avoid wasting employers' time with individuals who are not serious candidates and to preserve the privacy of an individual's career management or job-seeking activities.

5. Employers are contacted by a Job Bank USA recruiter within 48 hours of ordering a database search and are given the status of qualified, pre-screened candidates.

Who Pays and How Much?

Job seekers pay an annual fee of $30 to enroll in what the company terms the "Career Advancement Service." In addition to the database enrollment, the fee includes quarterly issues of a newsletter about job search trends and tips, and a catalog of career books and guidance materials. Employers pay for searches.

Type of Client Employers

More than 350 active client employers, ranging in size from major international corporations and Fortune 500 firms to regional and local employers, search the database.

How Do You Enter Your Resume?

Call and request an enrollment form. (Mention this book and receive a 10 percent discount.)

How Long Is a Resume Retained?

Enrollment forms are retained in the Job Bank USA database for one year. Many individuals renew their enrollments.

How Do You Revise Your Resume?

Each person enrolled in the Job Bank USA database is given a toll-free telephone number to use in making unlimited updates and changes to the enrollment form.

Other Facts

Job Bank USA says its philosophy favors long-term career management over short-term emergency job finding.

Job Bank USA is one of the most active resume database firms in operation. Positions are appropriate for experienced individuals seeking better jobs, recent college graduates, veterans transitioning into the civilian

Out of Uniform, into a Job

Resume databases can work effectively for long-distance searches, for newcomers, or for returning service personnel, as in the case of former U.S. Marine Lee Ann Bailey of Alexandria, Virginia.

Bailey says she found herself facing displacement after four years of service. Her most recent assignment was in California, but given the economic climate and difficulties of finding a position, she decided to return to her hometown on the East Coast to pursue employment in the private sector.

"I found retail sales positions to be in abundance; however, I felt the skills I acquired during my tenure in the Marine Corps were more suited to an accounting/administrative environment," says Bailey. "I pursued all available leads, including classified advertising, placement services, and local employment commission."

Bailey says an interviewer at the employment commission suggested she try Job Bank USA, a resume database service in McLean, Virginia.

"I called Job Bank USA and was provided with an overview of their services and was sent by mail an enrollment form to complete and return with my resume," Bailey recalls. "Within ten days of my enrollment being activated, I received three calls from one of the Job Bank USA recruiters."

During all telephone calls, Bailey was given a description of the position listed and the opportunity to consent to her resume being sent to a corporate client.

"Two of the positions presented to me were a comfortable match and I agreed to have my resume forwarded," says Bailey. "The position in which I was especially interested was with a large real estate organization—in its accounting department."

Bailey says she was happy to discover the real estate company also considered her a match and, after two interviews, she was offered the position.

"I recommend Job Bank USA to anyone searching for employment," said Bailey. "It proved to be a very effective career marketing resource."

market, work-ready persons with disabilities, returners to the job market, and others who have marketable skills.

▶ **MedSearch America:**   15254 NE 95th St.
Redmond, WA 98052
Telephone (206) 883-7252
Fax (206) 883-7465

Size and Type of Database

This is the best known healthcare resume database (and also healthcare job postings). MedSearch America is supported entirely by healthcare employers and recruitment agencies. It is primarily an online system, meaning accessed by computers although paper resumes are accepted. Job seekers should have at least two years' experience in health, a business background or other transferable skills, or specialized medical education/training. Some 1,500 resumes are entered in the database.

How the System Works

After your resume is inserted into the database, employer members search it and contact you if they're interested. The system is coded to maintain your confidential status.

Who Pays and How Much?

You can submit your resume by e-mail at no charge. To mail your resume, the first page is free, but there is a data input charge of $5 for each additional page. Mailed resumes should mention the area of the country where you wish to live, and include a 60-character title (including spaces) that summarizes your resume. Examples: "Medical technologist/2 yrs' exp/Chicago only" . . . "Physical therapist/3.5 yrs' exp/mgt exp/relo US"

Type of Client Employers

HMOs, PPOs, hospitals, medical schools, medical manufacturing companies, clinics, government and nonprofit organizations, healthcare associations, and pharmaceutical and biotech corporations. Examples: Johns Hopkins Hospital and Medical Center, FHP Healthcare, John Deere Healthcare, Department of Veterans Affairs, Project Hope, and Anderson Cancer Center.

How Do You Enter Your Resume?

Healthcare job seekers can mail or e-mail resumes. For online instructions on how to post your resume online, send e-mail to: howto-post@medsearch.com

How Long Is a Resume Retained?

Resumes remain online for 3 months.

How Do You Revise Your Resume?

You must resubmit the entire resume to be updated.

Other Facts

MedSearch America is a good example of a resume database that has expanded into a full-service niche resource—healthcare occupations. Job seekers with Internet access can also view nationwide healthcare job openings, interact with human resource managers and with other healthcare job seekers through online discussion groups. In addition, you can read healthcare industry and employment articles. MedSearch America is free to job seekers.

Of special interest is MedSearch America's Healthcare Recruiters Network. A single resume sent to this nationwide network of recruiters can make you visible for a wide spectrum of open and employer-paid positions. You must specifically request your resume to be posted on the Recruiters Network.

▶ **National Resume Bank:**   3637 4th Street North, No. 330
St. Petersburg, FL 33704
Telephone (813) 896-3694
Fax (813) 894-1277

Size and Type of Database

The National Resume Bank is an online resume database currently listing more than 3,000 job candidates in 35 different career categories.

How the System Works

1. The National Resume Bank is compatible with both IBM and Macintosh systems, and with 2400-baud modems.
2. The system is user-friendly and requires no special software.
3. Employers dial the National Resume Bank modem line (813) 822-7082 and select from 35 job categories the one that most closely describes the job opening. They can then select the geographic parameters desired (city, state, or national search).
4. Employers are shown a brief qualifications summary on each current job candidate who meets the search criteria.

5. Employers can contact the candidate directly or, with a key-stroke, order a paper copy of the candidate's resume. Candidates' personal information does not appear on screen; employer must request resume to get the data to contact candidate.

After an employer logs on to the system the first time, the database will recognize the company name for future searches. For example, an employer who may not wish to review every resume during each search can ask to see only the new listings since the last search.

Who Pays and How Much?

Job candidates pay $40 for unlimited time until they are employed or they request removal from the database. The service is free to employers.

Type of Client Employers

Because National Resume Bank does not require special employer software or charge prepaid, online, or download fees, the service is more accessible to small employers as well as to Fortune 500 companies. With 90 percent of new jobs being created by companies with fewer than 100 employees, the National Resume Bank says it is particularly user-friendly to this vast employment market.

The National Resume Bank is open to job applicants in 35 different categories:

Advertising/Public Relation

Aerospace

Airlines

Architecture

Casino (gaming)

Clerical

Communications

Computers/Data Processing

Creative

Data processing

Distribution

Education

Engineering/technical

Entertainment

Environmental

Financial

General

Government/public service

Health care

Hospitality

Human Resources

Insurance

International Business

Law Enforcement

Legal

Management

Manufacturing

Marketing

Medical

Purchasing

Real estate

Research

Retail

Sales

Social Sciences

Technical

Trades

(New categories may be added and current titles modified or deleted in response to future market needs and interests.)

How Do You Enter Your Resume?

Contact a local member of the Professional Association of Resume Writers (see your yellow pages directory), or mail five copies of your resume, include category and a 50 word qualification summary, along with the $40 listing fee to the address given above.

How Long Is a Resume Retained?

Each resume is kept for unlimited time until employed or requested to be removed. If files for resumes become empty, client has 30 days to replenish files or they are removed from database.

After each selected period on the database, the National Resume Bank mails database members a management report. The report notifies each job seeker how many times his or her listing was viewed by employers and how many times the full resume was requested.

At the same time, job seekers should be alert to direct contact by employers. A National Resume Bank listing no longer lists individuals name and phone number. Employer must request the resume to get that information.

How Do You Revise Your Resume?

This can be done at any time by sending National Resume Bank five copies of the new resume with a $5 update fee.

Other Facts

The National Resume Bank was begun in October 1991 as a new client service for members of the Professional Association of Resume Writers. It is designed to help job seekers present their qualifications and credentials to the 80 percent of employers who don't advertise their job openings in local classified ads.

During 1992 (National Resume Bank's first full year), listed resumes received more than 50,000 viewings by employers with current job openings.

▶ **Resume-Link:**   3972-C Brown Park Drive
Hilliard, OH 43026
Telephone (614) 777-4000
Fax (614) 771-5708

Size and Type of Database

Resume-Link's database program contains information on more than 20,000 degreed professionals with experience in the computer and engineering fields. The company inserts resumes from students and members of professional associations in more than 50 market-specific databases.

How the System Works

The resumes and profiles are received by Resume-Link from students and experienced workers. The information is entered into an easy-to-use computerized database, which employers can access on an annual subscription or single-search basis.

Who Pays and How Much?

Employers pay. The exception is nonmembers of a professional society in a market-specific database; for instance, if you are in the mechanical engineering database but don't belong to the profession's membership society, you pay about $50 a year.

Type of Client Employers

Companies employing engineers, pharmacists, and graduates with masters in business administration degrees.

How Do You Enter Your Resume?

Job seekers, usually members of professional associations, fill out a resume form, which is free of charge, and mail to Resume-Link.

How Long Is a Resume Retained?

Six months.

How Do You Revise Your Resume?

Telephone revisions or ask for a new resume form.

Other Facts

Resume-Link also produces electronic resume books for most of the top MBA programs as well as a number of undergraduate institutions. Colleges use this program to produce customized resume books and databases to help market their students to recruiters.

▶ **SkillSearch:**   3354 Perimeter Hill Drive
Suite 235
Nashville, TN 37211-4129
Telephone (615) 834-9448
Fax (615) 834-9453

Size and Type of Database

SkillSearch is a computerized career networking service linking college alumni and potential employers. The service is sponsored by more than 60 participating university alumni associations. SkillSearch targets all alumni of participating universities. The network's membership represents a complete range of experience, from junior level to seasoned executives.

How the System Works

1. Alumni are solicited directly by mail.
2. Participating alumni in the SkillSearch network complete an application that is transformed into a professional resume and unique data record.
3. The partnership with the participating university alumni associations provides SkillSearch with a database of skilled professionals ready to fill open positions.
4. Employers pay a fee for a database search that allows contact with up to 20 matching prospective candidates.
5. The employers select the profiles they wish to explore further.

Who Pays and How Much?

Alumni join SkillSearch for a one time fee of $65; renewals are $15 per year. Employers pay for a search of the database. If no matching candidates are found, the employer pays nothing.

Type of Client Employers

Fortune 1000 corporations, nonprofit organizations, and governmental agencies, as well as small- to medium-size companies, are clients of SkillSearch.

How Do You Enter Your Resume?

Alumni register with SkillSearch. Check with your office of alumni affairs for further information, or contact SkillSearch at the address given above.

How Long Is a Resume Retained?

Information remains in the database for one year and is renewable with payment of the annual fee.

How Do You Revise Your Resume?

Updates can be made as often as desired by notifying SkillSearch.

Other Facts

SkillSearch works only with alumni who have at least two years' work experience. The average is ten years. SkillSearch does not accept resumes from students.

▶   **University ProNet:**   2445 Faber Place
Box 51820
Palo Alto, CA 94303
Telephone: see below
Fax (415) 845-4019

Size and Type of Database

University ProNet is a private company wholly owned and operated by the 16 participating universities—all national leaders in the fields of business, engineering, science, law, medicine, and biotechnology. The database consists of 45,000 alumni of these universities.

The service is designed for professionals who have two or more years of experience. The preponderance of opportunities is in middle- to senior-level positions. Some 20 percent of individuals in the database are thought to be actively on the job market; 80 percent are open to career advancement moves.

More than 77 percent of individuals in the database hold advanced degrees, and more than 33 percent are currently employed as senior executives. Ten years is the median experience.

Participating institutions are: California Institute of Technology, Carnegie-Mellon University, Columbia University, Cornell University, Massachusetts Institute of Technology, Ohio State University, Stanford University, University of California at Berkeley, University of California at Los Angeles, University of Chicago, University of Illinois, University of Michigan, University of Pennsylvania, University of Texas at Austin, and Yale University.

Sources of Resumes

The database is restricted to alumni of participating universities.

How the System Works

1. Employers subscribe to the service on an annual basis. The level of subscription purchased determines the number of searches they can request.

2. When a search order is received, University ProNet personnel search the database and call likely candidates with whom to discuss the position.

3. Profiles of qualified alumni who are interested in the position—identified by code number only—are then forwarded to the client company.

4. The company identifies the specific candidates it would like to interview. At this point, University ProNet staff release to the company the

identity and contact information for each candidate and notify the candidates of the action.

5. Employers contact candidates directly. University ProNet staff now work as agents for the alumni, functioning as liaisons throughout the interviewing process.

To make its electronic service even more valuable, University ProNet publishes a twice-monthly resume book of alumni (different job seekers appear in each issue), and produces a twice-monthly printed job bulletin of employment opportunities apart from those filled through the electronic search system.

Who Pays and How Much?

Alumni are charged a lifetime fee of $35 to register in the program and be cross-matched against searches initiated by the subscribing companies.

Individuals who choose to have their profiles circulated in the resume book mailing and to receive the job bulletin for six months pay an additional $25.

Companies subscribe to University ProNet on an annual basis.

Type of Client Employers

A cross-section of business, financial, engineering, and consumer product corporations and organizations are clients.

How Do You Enter Your Resume?

University ProNet is a service of each school's alumni association to its alumni. Units are called, for example, Stanford ProNet or MIT ProNet. Alumni register by filling out a diskette supplied by their alumni association. The diskette contains a program that walks the registrant through an extensive history of education, work background, and skills base. The information collected on the standardized profile form is far more detailed than a traditional resume—a typical profile is six pages long.

To request information, alumni can call the following telephone numbers:

Cal ProNet (UC/Berkeley)	(800) 758-2326
Caltech ProNet (Calif. Inst. Tech.)	(800) 758-1944
Carnegie-Mellon ProNet (Carnegie-Mellon Univ.)	(800) 758-2696
Columbia University	(800) 593-3088
Cornell University	(800) 593-3084

Illinois ProNet (Univ. of Illinois)	(800) 593-3089
Michigan ProNet (Univ. of Michigan)	(800) 758-2644
MIT ProNet (Mass. Inst. of Technology)	(800) 758-2437
Ohio State ProNet (Ohio State Univ.)	(800) 758-1811
Stanford ProNet (Stanford Univ.)	(800) 726-0280
Texas ProNet (Univ. of Texas/Austin)	(800) 758-1626
UCLA ProNet (UCLA)	(800) 758-2104
University of Chicago	(800) 593-3085
Yale ProNet (Yale Univ.)	(800) 593-3086

If for any reason you must contact the service directly, use the address given on page 44.

How Long Is a Resume Retained?

If you update it annually, the resume remains in the database throughout your lifetime.

How Do You Revise Your Resume?

Each individual keeps a copy of his or her diskette, which can be used to revise a resume.

Other Facts

Started in 1987, University ProNet is the only database for university alumni operated by member institutions—it is not a third-party vendor. University ProNet does not work with executive search firms but only with employers and only on specific types of open positions. Individuals can block the release of their resumes to any number of companies.

▶ **V-Quest:**   5700 Fourth St. North
St. Petersburg, FL 33703
Telephone: (813) 528-4005
Fax (813) 528-4406

Size and Type of Database

V-Quest is a St. Petersburg-based online resume service launched in the fall of 1994, which presently has nearly 500 client companies.

How the System Works

For a fee, V-Quest offers the job seeker the opportunity to present his or her resume and profile to client companies who are looking for specific experiences and talents. The C-BOR System (computer-based online re-sume system) puts job candidate profile and resume information on the hiring manager's desk via computer.

Who Pays and How Much?

V-Quest charges the job seeker an annual membership fee of $79.95 ($6.66 per month) for their personal profile and resume to be entered onto the V-Quest C-BOR System for one year. There are no access charges to the client company.

Type of Client Employers

V-Quest's largest market is the academic field—colleges, universities, technical schools, etc. Underclassmen are encouraged to enter the V-Quest C-BOR System as well, allowing the soon-to-graduate an opportu-nity to test the job market, or in many cases, apply for internships that may lead to a permanent job upon graduation. V-Quest also is used by people already in the work force because of an attractive feature that al-lows the job seeker to block specific companies from gaining access to their file. This allows someone who is looking for a better job to do so without fear that their present employer will stumble across their file.

How Do You Enter Your Resume?

The job seeker completes a personal profile form on which they provide information regarding their job qualifications. The information they pro-vide, including their work history and experience, special skills, educa-tion, salary requirements and relocation preferences, along with their resume, are entered by V-Quest personnel onto the C-BOR System.

How Do You Revise Your Resume?

The job seeker also is provided an Applicant Profile Software Diskette, which allows them to update his or her profile and resume anytime dur-ing the membership year.

How Long Is a Resume Retained?

The job seeker's resume and profile remains on the system for one year, even if he or she has been hired, unless they request that their name be removed. The job seeker may remain on the system after one year "for a nominal fee," according to V-Quest officials.

3

Job Computers: Applicant Tracking Systems

Smart Software Is Changing the Way Hiring Happens in America—Here's What You Must Know

In the last chapter, we looked at **external** resume database services—services that inventory people.

In this chapter, we examine another way to inventory people—the new **internal** systems companies are using to electronically process their own pool of applicants whose unsolicited resumes come in "over the transom."

Today's front-running companies may use an external system, an internal system, or a combination of both.

Tracking systems are not exclusively for employers. Executive recruiters, who (for a fee) help client organizations find and appraise candidates for specific positions, also track applicants with these systems.

"We'll keep your resume on file." How many times have you heard that one?

The artfully constructed resume you pieced together dream by dream, tactic by tactic, and word by word is handed over to a corporate recruiter who, for all you know, orbits it into space. You never hear another word about it.

You've tried every trick in several books, from sending your resume to the company president claiming you both are alumni of the same university, to changing your status from job seeker to shareholder by buying one share of stock and asking the director of investor relations to pass your resume along.

Nothing is working, and the absence of a response is dashing your hopes and dreams. It happens time after time: the waiting, the anticipating. You begin to feel discouraged, frustrated, disheartened, rejected, depressed. What happened to those hundreds of resumes you sent? Doesn't anyone care? Why long-time-no-hear—from anyone?

A wall of silence is one of the real gut-wrenching complaints job seekers make about human resource specialists and hiring managers. You wonder: Why don't they have the common courtesy to acknowledge the receipt of your resume? Don't they remember what it was like when they were on the outside looking in?

You're not alone in having a pity party. Being ignored hurts. The discomfort you feel from being disregarded is largely because a resume mirrors *you*—it is a kind of proof of your individual existence, an edited portion of your life story. None of us actually expects to get a job offer from each and every employer to whom a resume is submitted, but we certainly expect acknowledgment that we exist.

Beyond mere wounded feelings, the underlying reason acknowledgment letters are so important is that high morale during a job search is essential to your success. Essential! When you are hammered by rejection—which is how you may subconsciously interpret the silent treatment—your sense of self-value begins to slip and you unknowingly broadcast messages of desperation: SOS . . . SOS.

Employers can smell despondency a mile away and will go to China and back to avoid it. Most managers try to be admirable people, but it's not their job to hire pitiful people with low self-esteem for whom they feel sorry. It's their job to hire winners.

The linkage of acknowledgment letters to the success of your job hunt is subtle, even obscure—and very real.

Why don't companies know this and get back to you promptly? The short answer is: staggering workloads.

Switch viewpoints, if you will, to the other side of the recruitment desk. Pity the poor beleaguered corporate recruiter who is told to find the best person for the job—fast!

As the recruiter stares at a room crowded with filing cabinets, which in turn are stuffed with paper resumes, a vague memory surfaces of a great resume of the perfect applicant. "Now let's see . . . where is it?"

No R.S.V.P.? Here's Why.

It's an old complaint from demoralized job hunters who have sent resumes in response to a recruitment ad:

"I am frustrated and disappointed by the insensitivity of human resource people. About half of the time, I hear nothing at all. Even when I do, the response is anything but prompt. It took one firm I applied to eight weeks to send me a rejection letter and another firm six weeks to tell me that they were not planning to fill the position after all. A third firm I've sent resumes to has failed to get back to me after five weeks."

It's sad but true: no one has your sense of urgency in your job hunt. This explains part of the time lag that seems an eternity when you're on the waiting end. Beyond that, is it really accurate to make a human resource person the villain of the piece?

Management experts say no, that it's scapegoating to lay the blame of no response or a slow response at the feet of human resource staff. The HR specialist is merely the focal point of the transaction and can act only when the hiring manager (or selection committee) makes a decision on the timing of the interviews. Unfortunately for job seekers, a hiring manager's attention to the employment process is not always a high priority.

Further delays arise when the work situation changes. Internal candidates may suddenly become available, budget problems may require a rethinking of hiring plans, a planned product introduction may be canceled, the word may get around that the company is being sold or relocated—any number of revised conditions can overnight alter the hiring process.

Not getting a response is even more likely when you send an unsolicited resume. Yes, a lack of acknowledgment is rude, but it's a fact of life in busy offices. Smart software systems can—and, we hope, will—change this part of the hiring process for the better.

Fifteen minutes later, no luck. The recruiter clearly remembers only that the perfect applicant's resume is filed away somewhere. Finding it will take forever and usually does.

The search may disintegrate as the recruiter tries to negotiate a landfill of paper. "Potential candidates who are highly qualified may be overlooked because their resume is misfiled—or lost on another hiring manager's desk," explains a corporate vice president of human resources who has looked for many needles in thousands of paper stacks.

Another human resource manager says finding the best employee for a job can be a dizzying, time-consuming, expensive process. "We used to have six people standing at copy machines all day," she explains. That was before her company found relief in electronic recruitment technology.

Because a mountain of paper can be a migraine to manage, leading-edge companies are turning to a raft of new software muscle programs to drive high-tech recruitment systems.

Not only do these electronic recruitment systems ride herd over resumes, they can be used for internal job posting in which, once you're employed, you can nominate yourself for a better job. The most sophisticated systems have a new feature: a telephone hotline permitting job applicants to call in and see if they're in the running for a given position. The job-status hotlines are still rare, but are likely to become more common within the next couple of years.

EXECUTIVE RECRUITERS FACE SAME PAPER MOUNTAINS

Executive search consultants, sometimes called executive recruiters or technical recruiters, decided in the 1970s that they'd had enough of paper farming. Once they had seen the joys of automation, they never looked back.

Executive search consultants are the hired hunters who stalk the best and brightest managerial and professional troops in the nation. Also called by the pejorative and informal title of "head-hunters," these talent seekers began to develop computer-driven resume databases and applicant tracking systems two decades ago. At first, the systems were on the primitive side. Today, the systems used by many of the search firms are as advanced as those in use at leading corporations. Other systems remain unsophisticated. It's a mixed bag.

If you're hoping to catch a recruiter's eye and be singled out from the crowd of hopefuls who want bigger and better jobs, pay close attention to this chapter and to our companion book, *Electronic Resume Revolution.*

A search consultant literally searches outward, gathering leads from many sources. But contemporary executive search firms maintain internal applicant tracking systems alongside their subscriptions to electronic resume databases of candidates, compiled from various sources.

When a likely name turns up, the search consultants are soon on the telephone checking out the lead.

When you want a recruiter to discover you, to tap you on the shoulder with a sword and raise you to the heights of corporate nobility, get into as many databases as possible. This includes those of professional societies, trade associations, and college alumni. A companion smart move is to get into as many recruiters' applicant tracking systems as possible.

To identify search consultants, check the annual *Directory of Executive Recruiters* (Kennedy and Kennedy, Inc., Fitzwilliam, NH).

APPLICANT TRACKING SYSTEMS EASE PAPER OVERLOAD

Whether business or politics was the cause, organizations that hire people have awakened to a new realization: They somehow must change the way work gets done if they are to meet the goal of achieving more productivity and profit with fewer people and costs. They must change—or they won't survive.

If you've been active in the job market recently, you know that, for many organizations, the decade of the 1990s has been one of stress and struggle.

When employers find out they can use job computers to significantly reduce costs and improve the quality and efficiency of their employment function, they're saying, "Let's do it."

And the word is getting out fast. Simply put, to make the employment situation manageable, internal applicant tracking systems—more easily called job computers—have become an integral part of the way large corporations—and, increasingly, midsize companies—do business.

What about companies that are too small to have their own internal systems? They are starting to buy time on systems operated by commercial firms, the applicant tracking service bureaus.

Whether an employer is filling jobs from external independent resume databases or from an internal applicant tracking system, the implications for you, the job seeker or career self-manager, are enormous.

There's no doubt about it: The new intelligent software technology sweeping America has both a dramatic upside and a troubling downside.

RESUME AUTOMATION: THE UPSIDE

Communication

For those times when you do not receive an immediate job offer, resume software technology certainly is better mannered than traditional manual processing systems. It permits human resource specialists, with very little effort, to let you know your resume made it to their desks.

Most applicant tracking systems, with the click of a mouse or the stroke of a key, can generate a letter saying "We'll keep your resume on file." But these employment managers are not merely banging a kettledrum of little white lies.

They mean it because computers have made resume databases possible; they are a form of new human resource wealth.

Once a nuisance, resumes are now warmly welcomed because every hire from a company's own resume bank is one less expense to farm out to employment services or recruitment advertising. It's like saving money by eating in rather than dining out.

Inclusion

There is another benefit to having a computer read your resume. The machine can provide the break you need to get into the running. When the economy thunders down too many resumes on a human resource department, a normally good system can be reduced to a 90-pound weakling.

Instead of a screening by an experienced employment manager, the initial resume task may be a sorting dumped on untrained clerical workers.

Typically, these inexperienced aides are told to sort in three stacks: "yes" for a current opening, "future possibles" for a later one, and "no interest" for those documents that will be unceremoniously snuffed.

If the clerical screener doesn't understand what your resume says— and finds some technical resumes are as mystifying as the Dead Sea

Scrolls—you're history. Worse, if the clerical screener happens to harbor a bias that works against you, your resume is dead on arrival.

Fairness

By contrast, the argument can be made that the early winnowing process is more meticulous—and fairer—when performed by computer reasoning than by humans.

Computers, even when guided by expert systems and artificial intelligence, don't move away from their "factory installed" overall guidelines. Humans, shaped by differing life experiences, may unknowingly screen with bias or ignorance.

Bias can enter the picture at any stage of human intervention, but if a computer is on the job, you'll probably get past its electronic sentry and into the database. Once in, you'll have a chance of being pulled out for hiring consideration.

Returning to the issue of fairness, companies have a practical reason to support objective recruitment and promotion policies: Employers that discriminate are sitting ducks for legal nightmares and severe financial penalties.

"The very nature of resume automated systems enhances evenhandedness," says an employment manager whose department has been using an applicant tracking system for more than a year. "Most programs produce a list of all appropriate candidates in ranked order, based on the predetermined values assigned to job skills," he adds.

"Systems can be used to electronically store resumes that have been 'sanitized' of any inappropriate information, such as age, gender, race, and disability," he explains.

(After hiring takes place, the data removed by sanitizing can be reshuffled electronically to instantly produce mandated equal employment opportunity and affirmative action reports for companies holding federal contracts.)

Multi-Opportunities

Another positive note for resume software technology is that once inside it, your resume automatically casts a wider net.

By the use of keywords, you are considered for every job opening within striking distance of your abilities.

When you are preparing a paper resume, you may choose to place early in the document a summary of your qualifications. Depending on the circumstances, it's often advisable to lead off with a fairly well-defined objective so that resume readers will know to which occupational tribe you belong.

Employers have a habit of speed reading and can skim a resume in ten seconds flat. By eliminating the guesswork of how you would fit into an organization, you position yourself to be chosen.

With computers, an employer is not forced to wade through your resume trying to decide whether your qualifications will wrap around the job's requirements or essential functions. These well-oiled hiring machines may find your name in any of several categories, rather than in just one.

You may, for instance, jump to the recruiter's screen as a candidate for *mechanical engineer,* or *manager with five years' experience,* or *quality control specialist.* Maybe you'll even turn up in the *technical writing* category as well.

Now suppose you're an A-1 mechanical engineer and you wrote the book on quality control, but you have only two years' managerial experience and writing isn't your strong point.

In a search with the descriptors given above, your name may surface and you'll make the first cut. But you probably will fade away if the database is rich with better qualified candidates.

(There are no guarantees in electronic hide-and-seek. It's like a poker game: You don't know what cards the other players are holding.)

You're an intelligent person—you know that no one will hire you as a technical writer. What's more, you lack more than half the requested managerial experience. So what good does it do, you ask, to make the first cut?

The benefit of being nominated—of being yanked out of electronic oblivion—is that you have a fighting chance to wind up in someone's office for an interview. Getting inside is always better than being locked outside. It's that simple.

Employers don't always know exactly what they want when they write job requisitions. They may ask for ten "requirements" and, depending on the pool of applicants, settle for someone they like who has only seven of the requirements, particularly when compensatory strengths can be plugged into the gaps.

Speed

An advantage of applicant tracking systems is the speeded-up timetable they make possible. Before the 1980s, an employment manager shopping for the most qualified members of the available work force might have used a manual system no more sophisticated than graphpaper chart comparisons of candidates' qualifications.

Down the left side of the sheet were the candidates' names. Along the top of the page were specifications of the job. Checkmarks or numerical rankings were jotted down after each candidate's name.

The employment manager and the hiring manager sometimes met and reviewed the listing, often many pages long. They selected the most promising candidates and studied their resumes, cover letters, letters of reference, and other material, trying to rank the applicants in a descending order of most qualified to least qualified.

An employment manager for a major brewery that receives 40,000 job applications a year says, "After half an hour of juggling applications and trying to keep 10 or 15 candidates' information in mind, the managers' brain may be in a morass."

Now that resumes can be scanned and automatically sorted and ranked (by preprogrammed values for each job specification), the process is almost as simple and fast as 1-2-3, *click!* We call the process "resume surfing" because it's designed to catch the best waves of candidates. Resume surfing takes about 1.5 seconds per page, and ranking doesn't take much longer. Making faster decisions about whom to interview hurries the hiring process along.

Technology may not hurry the hiring decision along. The action steps are in the human realm of control, and you know what that means. The actual choice of a candidate and the start date for a new hire may drag out for reasons quite beyond the scope of computers.

Bull's-Eye Matching

Another plus for resume automation is that you need not, ever again, hear that unpopular "O" word. Being told repeatedly that you are "overqualified" for a position may be true, but it's also a synonym for age discrimination.

If a job really is below your capabilities, you shouldn't be interviewing for it. The computer won't let you be called in only to suffer one more rejection in a personal interview.

Understanding the String-Along Game

Despite the fast start that smart software gives to the employment process, speedy hiring isn't always the outcome. Why do job seekers experience interminable waiting for a firm offer to come through, even when employment or hiring managers have indicated interest?

Sometimes, the answer is simple: They hate to say no. At other times, the answer is complex: It could be any of a million reasons. So the managers stall and string you along:

"We want to hire you, but we have to get the paperwork from the regional office."

"We need to see a few more people before we can do the deal, but personally I'm pulling for you."

"We're having a great quarter. When a business pickup is solid, the hiring freeze should end."

Some string-alongs actually are true. So what? The end result for you is still zero.

Among signs that a string-along has some degree of truth: Your references may be contacted, or a hiring manager may put a time frame on the conversation, "If you don't hear from HR this week, call me."

Still, these signs are not a paycheck. Even after a verbal offer, the situation can fall apart, leaving you with a loss of job and a lack of momentum. The lesson to be learned is that you, as a prudent person, must continue your all-out job hunt until the day you report to work.

The flip side is that if you really want the job and you are willing to take steps backward to get it, you won't be given the chance to persuasively plead your case. You may not have to hear the "O" word, but you may have to read it in a regret letter that describes how your skills overshoot the position.

Other boons of computer-driven applicant tracking may become apparent as the systems grow, but one other point jumps out: It's time to take a new look at broadcast letters.

Makes Cold-Calling Cost-Effective

Broadcast letter writing is cold-calling by mail. You compile a list of companies and organizations that could hire you for the kind of work you want, and you send out a mass mailing of your resume with a cover letter.

Many career specialists are lukewarm on this strategy. They believe it is costly and ineffective to mass mail to a large universe of employers without very careful preparation and selection.

Now that applicant tracking systems encourage electronic storage of resumes, sometimes for years or a lifetime, mailing even a few resumes may be well worth your time and postage. As a practical matter, well-done broadcast mailing is no longer a one-time shot, but a kind of investment in your career.

RESUME AUTOMATION: THE DOWNSIDE

The biggest problems intelligent software systems create for job seekers are described here.

Excludes All but Top Picks

The systems skim the cream off the crop of applicants, taking the best and leaving the rest. That's okay if you're at the top of the list.

If you're not, you must find ways to get around the system, such as human networking—using all your personal contacts to get fair consideration.

Machine Error

Scanning equipment can malfunction or misread your document, leaving your resume out in left field. You can't do much about this. But if you never seem to be among the chosen, it's worth reviewing your resume to be sure it's clean copy that isn't giving scanners and optical character recognition software fits.

Salary Buster

Perhaps the most distressing problem is that some automated resume systems sharply reduce your salary negotiating power.

What Happens When You Apply Three Times to the Same Company?

One area of job search that is ripe for rethinking is the practice of submitting multiple resumes and cover letters to the same employer, especially resumes that are customized to fit a particular position.

The old advice still holds for companies that use manual systems: Tailor your approach for each position. Try to match your qualifications point-by-point with the specifications of the position.

In the accounting field, for instance, you might emphasize your international auditing experience for a position with responsibilities beyond U.S. borders, but, two months later, remake your resume for the same employer to focus on your electronic data processing auditing skills. Still later, you may see that the same company is advertising a position for an accountant with internal auditing experience. You have that too, so you rush back to your word processor and print out a third resume that headlines your internal auditing experience. All three resumes are true; each reflects a facet of your background, depending on the job opening. You have engaged in situational resume writing, tilting each resume toward the target job opening.

For processing in sizable manual systems, situational resume writing is good strategy. The chances are slim that all three documents will turn up on the same desk, particularly if they are submitted over a period of months.

By contrast, for processing in electronic systems, situational resume writing may or may not be good strategy. Here's why.

When your resume is scanned into a company's database, theoretically you are considered each time an electronic search ferrets out appropriate candidates. Supposedly, you need not reapply for each new opening in which you're interested. The computer should poke around and find out that your qualifications are relevant when you are a potentially good match for a job opening.

But because of the possibility, however remote, that scanning equipment will misread, miscode, or even eat your resume,

What Happens When You Apply Three Times to the Same Company? (cont.)

it's probably a good idea to resubmit a resume to the same company for each job you want.

When you customize your resume for each opening (situational resume writing), the issue becomes iffy. The idea is similar to saying more or less the same thing to each person in serial interviews—perhaps six people from the same company may interview you at separate times. You must come across as the same person in all of your resumes that reside in the same internal database.

This is particularly important when dealing with executive recruiters, most of whom have databases.

Again, assuming a trio of resumes, try to emerge as the same person on each document. Chances are very high that the computer will flag all three resumes, making it easy for a screener to compare them. The screener may think, "First this woman said her strong suit was international auditing. Next she says she's a whiz at EDP auditing. Then she positions herself as an internal auditor. Sounds like resume inflation to me."

If you submit multiple resumes, take pains not to be seen as an individual who plays games with your qualifications.

We're in favor of multiple resumes and situational resume writing—as long as the truth isn't stretched to the point of misrepresentation. Sending new paper each time you apply for different positions at the same company is wise. Just as computers are not infallible, human resume screeners may misjudge or lose your resume, or there may be new people, or the job requirements may change.

Even if a trio of your resumes does turn up on the screen or in the same file folder, it probably won't hurt your chances or project you as being desperate for employment. An equally likely supposition is that you're really interested in the company and deserve to be interviewed.

With good reason, most job hunt guides urge you to do advance research on where you want to work. The more you know

(continued)

What Happens When You Apply Three Times to the Same Company? (cont.)

about a prospective employer, the more easily you can show how your credentials match a position's requirements.

In this new era of electronic job search, add one more item to your research list: Has the company yet switched to an internal applicant tracking system?

If so, keep records and make sure all your resumes are written on the same music sheet even though the lyrics are different.

The salary issue is a constant problem, for a number of reasons. None of them is easy to solve. When electronic recruitment technology meets the salary issue, the problem gets worse. Here's what we mean.

If you have been reading job hunt guides, you know:

1. *It is in your best interests* not *to discuss salary until a job offer has been made.* Once you know a company wants you, the negotiation is between parties with virtually equal power. Until a job offer comes, the employer is calling the shots and is in total control. The employer owns all the uniforms, bats, and balls, and you're not even on first base.

2. *Until you talk through the position, you don't know what the work is worth.* You need to know the job's details. If you agree to a price prematurely, you're buying, with your labor, into a new ball game you know very little about—not a good move.

These are two good reasons why it's an error to state on your resume either your salary history or the salary you expect. You probably know what pay you'd like to have or what you need to pay the bills, but that isn't necessarily your market value.

Research to find out what you're worth in the job market, and fight hard to get it. Even if you've been underpaid for a while, this is difficult but manageable. (See *Dynamite Salary Negotiations: Know What You're Worth and Get It!* by Drs. Ronald L. and Caryl Rae Krannich, Impact Publications, 1994.)

Your original resume or a skills profile may have no salary information, but you may still be asked to supply salary history or expectations on a supplemental form. This is not to your advantage, but there's little you can do other than comply.

View a call for salary history or expectations not as a request but as a command. When a computer is told to pull names of applicants—say, managers in the $40,000 to $50,000 bracket—it won't find you if you have ducked the issue by writing "Will discuss" in the space where you're asked about money.

(The "Will discuss" answer often works fine in human reviews of applicants, but not well at all when computers read your application.)

Another salary buster occurs when your salary identity dwells in a database over a period of years and becomes out-of-date. You will have grown professionally and will be qualified to earn more money, but a resume lodged in an in-house system won't reflect that fact unless you remember to send in an updated resume.

You probably have some reservations about having your personal financial data float around where any employee with a password can spy it out. According to makers of applicant tracking systems, access to confidential data and specific functions is restricted to authorized users. True? Untrue?

Here's one job-seeking manager's opinion: "I may be unduly cynical but I read the same news stories about computer hackers breaking into CIA computers that you do."

The privacy issue remains to be proven employer-by-employer, but the plain truth is that electronic resume databases are here to stay. Let's see how a representative in-house system actually functions in a company.

HOW A JOB COMPUTER WORKS

Each of the major internal applicant tracking systems offers varying performance features.

Some offer blow-you-away sophistication and virtuosity in preparing every human resource report a company could possibly want. Others are less ambitious. All of them provide similar functions in a new recruiting frontier.

These are the journey legs as your resume voyages through a database.

Scanning

Your original resume—the one you labored at writing, or paid dearly to have written—is welcomed into the applicant tracking system's database by the amazing scanning and optical character recognition technology mentioned earlier. The technology reads and absorbs its contents, adding your resume to a huge computerized pool of job talent.

Your credentials may be sorted and stored in a number of ways, including alphabetically, regionally, or by specialty skills. An example is given in Figure 3–1.

Dating

The software automatically stamps the date on your records, which will later show when your resume was received and entered.

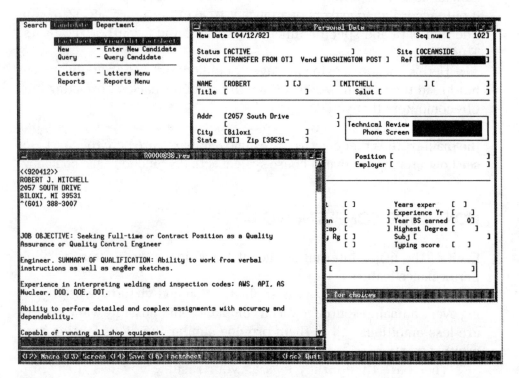

Figure 3–1   Computer Screen Produced by Applicant Tracking System.
(Courtesy of SmartSearch2/Advanced Personnel Systems, Inc., Oceanside, CA)

Being polite as well as smart, the software now says, "It's time to confirm that we received this applicant's resume," and an acknowledgment letter goes out. It too is date-stamped.

Requisition Tracking

The hiring manager issues (through the human resource department) a job requisition to the system. Upon receipt of the requisition, the system switches over to a "requisition tracking" mode—and is off and running on an electronic sprint to find "best match" candidates.

Most tracking systems have predefined categories, such as education and industry experience. They are accessed automatically.

The hiring manager can ask for other categories specific to the position, such as the ability to use a specific brand of graphic-design software or to analyze toxic air samples. By inserting keywords, the search can be tailored to a gnat's eyebrow. The process is called "building a search." It means matching the exact specifications of a job requisition with the credentials of applicants in the database.

Weighting Keywords

The hiring manager, through the use of a sliding scale, can weight each predefined category or tailored keyword according to its level of importance.

For example, the descriptors used in the search may call for an "engineering technician" who has a two-year "associate degree," but may give preference to an "engineering technologist" who holds a four-year "bachelor's degree." The technician must either live in or be willing to move to "St. Louis, MO." The information from the categories will be "matched" with any and all resumes in the system that fit the job requisition.

In this overview, let's assume your resume fits the job requisition and is still in the running. The tracking system has zeroed in on the following matching keywords in your resume:

- *Personal data*—your name, address, home and work telephone numbers, planning data for equal employment opportunity and affirmative action policies, residence status and willingness to relocate and travel.

- *Skills data*—your skills and related proficiencies.
- *Education data*—schools you attended (and the dates), field of study, degrees and certificates earned, licenses and permits held, and professional association memberships.
- *Prior experience*—your previous employers, usually with the present or last being placed first; position titles, salaries, duties, scope of authority, number of people managed, sales records, and the like.
- *Employment testing*—job test dates and results (the system can track these).
- *Applicant contact*—records of all communications and contacts with you, from initial acknowledgment of your resume's receipt to interview schedules or acceptance/regret letters.

Ranking

If you're tapped electronically to become a "screen star," the software will, within seconds, add your candidacy to others similarly qualified and present you within a ranked list.

In many cases, the human resource specialist or hiring manager views your original resume, along with the capsule of data pulled out from the resume (called an applicant summary or an extracted summary), on a computer monitor.

In some systems, your information is stored in an online database in three versions:

1. A capsule of name, rank, serial number, and categories into which you fit;
2. An applicant summary from the original resume, or a skills profile (a standardized form that makes comparisons easier);
3. An exact image of your resume.

The data in any or all versions are instantly available to a resume reader.

Even in less complex tracking systems, the resume reader can select an individual name on the computer screen's matching display and bring up the entire resume. Usually, these tracking systems will highlight (electronically illuminate) on the screen the precise specifications that qualify the resume for the requisition. This feature gives the searcher an instant grasp of how each candidate matches the job requisition, and makes it easy to see how, "on screen" at least, you fit the job.

Qualified candidates are listed according to how each person matches the requisition. The best matches appear at the top of the computer screen; the fewest matches are at the bottom.

The relative score of each candidate appears as a number next to the candidate's name on the ranked list. As an example, those with "bachelor degree" will be listed ahead of those with "associate degree" if that's what the search dictates.

In the earlier search for an engineering technologist willing to move to St. Louis, resumes from that city will be listed ahead of other geographic locations, providing all other categories are equal.

Publishing

The electronic genie can be told to conjure up any or all of the information about you and your competitors in hard (print) copy, faxes, or e-mail.

In a flash, the searcher can send the selected resumes to be run out on laser printers or by fax to hiring managers across the hall or across the nation. Let's hope you're among the favored.

Cross-Searching

In a slightly different scenario, your name may not come up as the result of a newly ordered job requisition search, but as a possible answer to some unfinished business.

Not infrequently, a department manager spends months searching high and low for the perfect candidate for a hard-to-fill position. The manager has left a standing order to call when/if the perfect person comes along. Let's assume you're that perfect person. When your resume is scanned into the system, a flare goes up, alerting the manager that the human resource department may have struck pay dirt.

As you can see, the possibilities of a resume tracking system are vast and potentially rewarding for your job search. But when you get a warm and friendly customized letter acknowledging your resume, don't get too confident just yet. The signature on your letter really wasn't handwritten. It was generated automatically from the system's image memory of personalized signatures. Amazing, these machines.

TOMORROW'S CUTTING-EDGE TECHNOLOGY TODAY

Constantly aware of keen competition and a thirst for even more applications, software companies continue to upgrade and innovate their programming. To remain competitive in a rapidly growing market of employers, innovation is urgent.

Putting the electronic recruitment issue into perspective, a director of corporate human services management recently said management demands swift solutions in today's market, and the question for employment managers in the 1990s isn't "to scan or not to scan," but rather "to compete or not to compete." In the not too distant future, it will be normal practice in American industry for resumes to be read by computer.

(For the job seeker in the 1990s, perhaps the question isn't "to learn computer job search or not to learn computer job search," but rather "to compete or not to compete.")

We have identified a number of applicant tracking software systems currently being used by corporate America. More companies appear yearly. Nearly all of these applicant tracking systems basically work the same way, but each has at least one or two distinctions, a few of which are substantial.

Most applicant tracking systems process resume information by digesting the entire contents of the document. However, some copy the exact image of the resume being scanned and some don't. Although the first approach takes up a lot more computer memory, some human resource managers say having an exact copy of an applicant's resume on their screen can be helpful with judging the following criteria:

- *The way an applicant lays out a resume.* The hiring specialist or manager may want an advance look at the applicant's organizational qualities and neatness. How carefully designed and complete is the original resume?
- *The way an applicant spells and uses grammar.* This speaks for itself.
- *An applicant's use of a professional resume service.* Some human resource specialists abhor professionally prepared resumes because they look as though they rolled off an assembly line and often are so overproduced that they project Madison Avenue puffery. Human resource specialists may wonder why the applicant needs such heavy packaging if he or she is such hot stuff.

Still other hiring specialists and managers couldn't care less who prepared the resume.

There is another advantage in having the exact copy of the resume in the database: Some factual detail on the resume may not be captured by job computers that rearrange the resume into a standardized format.

An applicant may list information that gives an interviewer some insight into his or her personality—for example, something signifying risk taking, such as "skydiving" as a hobby—but that information probably would never be known if the actual resume were not retrieved for viewing.

The overall goals of any job computer is to be fast, consistent, and thorough, and to give every job seeker the same treatment.

Applicant tracking software can provide employers with unbiased candidate evaluation procedures and with effective, detailed record-keeping systems. For example, a job computer can make it much easier to document compliance with government employment requirements, when necessary.

A spokesperson for Bell Atlantic, a 73,000-plus employee corporation with a number of subsidiaries nationwide, says her office receives an average of 75,000 to 100,000 unsolicited resumes a year.

"We're trying to hold that number down, but it tends to go up and down with the economy," says the spokesperson. "We attempt to limit our unsolicited resumes from applicants not likely to be good matches through using an 800 number that details company requirements."

Bell Atlantic hires more than 500 professional and technical personnel annually, and another 5,000 to 6,000 nonexempt employees, including temporary and part-time workers.

"We used to hire a lot of college graduates right out of school, but we're hiring more seasoned veterans now than we used to," she says. "We formerly hired a lot of entry-level workers so that we could train them internally, but now we look for more experienced, job specific knowledge, people who can 'hit the ground running.'"

She explains that her company utilizes three types of scanning and imaging: (1) image character recognition, (2) intelligent character recognition, and (3) optical mark recognition.

Job seekers applying for nonexempt positions at Bell Atlantic usually do not submit a resume. Instead, they fill out an application, which is scanned with an intelligent character recognition system that converts the handwritten application into a basic resume, according to the spokesperson.

The applicant tracking system then handles this basic resume much like it would handle submitted resumes, only on a different level of hiring requirements.

As for all other job seekers submitting resumes, the spokesperson says Bell Atlantic no longer keeps the paper once the resume has been scanned into the company's database in Arlington, Virginia.

"That was a big step forward in gaining valuable filing space," says the spokesperson. "It's [the applicant tracking system] not only reduced the working space we need, but we've significantly reduced the staff we used to need in the human resources department." She adds that being able to operate in less space amounts to a significant savings because of the high price tag on office space in the major metropolitan areas where the company operates.

Bell Atlantic has taken the art of electronic applicant tracking even further. It has developed a system that interacts with Resumix and allows any employee of the telecommunications company to access a special 800 telephone number to inquire what jobs are available within the company.

"You need your social security number and a special company PIN [personal identification number] in order to access the system," explains the spokesperson. "This is to keep independent recruiters from getting into the system to take advantage. This program is strictly for our employees."

Once the system is accessed via a push-button telephone, she notes, the employee can either apply right on the phone for the job desired, or request a more detailed job description for the opening.

"We fax the job description directly to the employee. Most workers have access to a company fax," she observes. "Faxing is less expensive than using either internal mail or the U.S. mail system, according to an internal study."

She says that, during a typical week, 6,000 to 8,000 employee calls come into the in-house job openings system. In turn, about 1,000 faxes are sent, detailing anywhere from 200 to 400 positions that are open.

"We hire inside among our existing employees whenever possible," the Bell Atlantic spokesperson explains.

She adds that nonexempt employees (workers who legally must be paid at overtime rates for overtime work) can arrange for a standing application (the application remains in place until an advertised position is

So Much for Australia . . .

After being laid off from his defense industry job at Northrop Corporation in the Los Angeles area, computer whiz James Blanton figured the timing was right for him to see a bit of the world. Why not work his way around the globe? Why not start in Australia? Blanton began searching for an Australian employer who needed his skills.

"I bought this job search book listing foreign employment opportunities and there were a lot of listings for Australian companies," says Blanton. "A friend of mine was helping me mail out applications. I asked her to send my resume to all the companies listed in Australia."

Two weeks later, Blanton says, he received a call from San Francisco-based Bank of America. Unaware of exactly who had been sent his resume, Blanton quickly found out that among the companies listed in Australian opportunities was Bank of America.

"I guess they have some sort of operation there," he says. "Anyway, when they called, we scheduled a meeting. I was offered a job about a week after the interview."

Blanton accepted a systems engineering position in computer security—not in Australia, but at Bank of America's Concord (California) Technical Center, just east of Oakland, California.

What happened was this: Blanton's mailed resume had been received and placed into the company's computerized applicant tracking system, which quickly tagged it as matching the requirements for one of the bank's technical openings.

Blanton says he isn't aware of what sort of system the human resource department uses, but he sure is pleased with its results.

"I couldn't be happier with the way things worked out," says Blanton.

And Australia?

"Well, I have a pen pal in New Zealand who gave me the idea of going down under in the first place, but that's on the back burner now," Blanton says as he glances appreciatively at a picture of the Golden Gate Bridge on his wall.

filled). This ensures that the interested employee is considered for that job without needing to call every day or every week to check on its status.

San Francisco-based Bank of America, California's largest and one of the nation's biggest financial institutions, uses a major applicant tracking system, which officials at the bank prefer not to name. A spokesperson for Bank of America's Systems Engineering Group in San Francisco has a staff of ten human resource specialists and recruiters to service the division.

"This applicant tracking system allows us to become our own personnel agency," the spokesperson explains. "We get our resumes and applications from a variety of sources: media advertising, career fairs, internal transfers, and computer networks."

The Systems Engineering Group spokesperson says his division, which has more than 4,000 workers, receives an average of 150 resumes weekly. "It can be as high as 400 to 500 a week, depending upon how many ads we've run in the media," he adds.

"We put resumes in file folders before going to this system four years ago," the spokesperson recalls. He says automated tracking has proven itself. "We're committed to the applicant tracking system. And the other divisions are watching our progress closely and with great interest."

The Systems Engineering Group generally hires between 350 to 400 people per year. "That includes the transfers from within our employee ranks," explains the spokesperson. He says the applicant tracking system has allowed more efficiency in his department.

"We've not only downsized in personnel, but where our old manual way would require five recruiters to handle 150 [position] openings, today three recruiters handle 200 openings," he notes. "We certainly can do a much higher volume of work with fewer people because of this system."

The spokesperson finds it fascinating that a computerized applicant tracking system allows the first two or three steps of the job hiring process to be accomplished "automatically" without human assistance.

"One thing it [the system] can't do, though, is speak directly to the candidate to get an even closer match for the final hiring," he concludes. "You can't take the human factor out of this."

PRC, Inc., of McLean, Virginia, a professional services company that does 75 percent of its business with the federal government, uses job computers. An employment manager for PRC says his company has more than 25,000 resumes scanned into the database.

"We receive about 20,000 resumes yearly," says the manager, who was with the company before it installed job computers. "It's a real time-saver. The number of work hours we've saved is significant."

The manager says until he was appointed to head his department's applicant tracking process, no one really had a handle on just how much time was saved.

His department has about 15 human resource specialists who use the system daily to handle the many job requisitions that come from PRC managers monthly.

"This type of programming is really in its infancy," the manager explains. "It is very important to implement the system properly to take advantage of all its capabilities."

WHO MAKES APPLICANT TRACKING SYSTEMS?

A number of applicant tracking systems is available to companies and recruiting firms. *Resumix* in Santa Clara, California (owned by the Ceridian Corporation in Minneapolis, Minnesota) is the largest vendor. It is the same industry as *Restrac* in Deham, Massachusetts, *SmartSearch2* (Advanced Personnel Systems) in Oceanside, California, and *AbraTrak* (Abra Cadabra Human Resource Software) in St. Petersburg, Florida.

Talent Network Inc., in Prospect Park, New Jersey, operates *R2A* (Remote Resume Access) as a human resources service bureau that manages resume files for corporate clients. Advanced Personnel Systems (above) also operates a service bureau for companies that wish to outsource their electronic resume databases. Other entrepreneurs have contacted the authors saying they are operating as resume-scanning service bureaus for midsize and small companies.

Advanced Personnel Systems, Inc. has two main business offerings. The first, *SmartSearch2,* supplies employers with internal applicant tracking systems.

The second, *SS2 OnLine,* provides a service bureau. Previously, companies wishing to implement effective applicant tracking programs had to buy computer systems. Even with modern scanning-based systems, the data entry chore may be too much and that's why hundreds of companies outsource their resume scanning function to SS2 OnLine.

In a new wrinkle, Advanced Personnel Systems is the first to go on the Internet and remove all the road blocks in the transmission of resumes from sender to employers. In short, there are no technical buttons to push; it just happens. The format is titled the "SS2 OnLine Job Fair."

Here's how the Job Fair works. Companies post their job openings on the Internet. (The service is free to APS client employers; for a fee to non-APS clients. The fee pays for converting resumes into a format that flows smoothly into existing applicant tracking systems.)

As job seekers read the job postings and send in their resumes, the resumes immediately become available to recruiters and can be checked against *all* open job requisitions.

For general information on the SS2 OnLine Job Fair, send e-mail to: info@aps.com. To view the SS2 OnLine Job Fair on the Internet World Wide Web: http://www.aps.com/Welcome.html.

In the first edition of this work, we listed a dozen or so vendors of applicant tracking software to illustrate their existence. We were proving that resumes are being managed electronically—an unfamiliar notion at the time. Two years later we have discovered so many similar products— a majority of which are used primarily be small recruiting firms—that we've decided to forgo a comprehensive listing. As a practical matter, it doesn't directly help job seekers to know the names and addresses of the entire job computer industry.

By contrast, human resource specialists and recruiters who do want to know all the products in the marketplace before comparison-shopping for a system can identify competitive job computer software by reading advertisements in professional employment and personnel publications.

THE WAVE OF THE FUTURE

Applicant tracking systems are where the big action is in the electronic recruitment revolution.

A Texas systems manager puts it into perspective when he says human resource personnel are not functioning in a radically different way from manual systems, but they are "functioning more quickly and efficiently. It's like trading in a horse for a car."

4 Armchair Job Hunting

Online Ads and Career Resources That Jump onto Your Computer Screen

In the last two chapters, we examined databases that contain resumes—people.

In this chapter, we look at the jobs side. The blistering speed with which the Internet has moved into the job arena is rocketing the numbers of classified help-wanted ads available by computer—and spotlighting the entire career development process.

The Internet, the global network of networks, has become so powerful a medium during the past two years that one of the authors wrote an entire book about it (*Hook Up, Get Hired! The Internet Job Search Revolution* by Joyce Lain Kennedy; John Wiley & Sons).

We do not duplicate that book in this chapter, but the entire scope of online job finding and career development has become so exciting that we do give you a thumbnail sketch of what you can expect with armchair job hunting.

To begin, the Internet represents stunning empowerment for the job seeker. Online search is the most liberating, most important benefit for job seekers in the past six decades—since the end of World War II. Why? In times past, you could reach out and touch perhaps a dozen new people in one meeting; on the Internet you can show your stuff before hundreds of thousands of potential employers and employment allies. Until now, you had to manually search through the recruitment ads—now, you can tell the computer what you want and it searches for you, pulling up only your target ads. Moreover, you can get through to people by e-mail that you couldn't hope to reach on the telephone.

In an increasingly complex world and a chaotic job market, electronics comes to the rescue in the drive to uncover job leads.

No matter how splendiferous your resume or superb your interviewing skills, your challenge is to search out and pinpoint where the jobs are.

In sales work, this task is like developing a prospect list. In fund raising, it's creating a contributor base. In politics, it's identifying the committed voters. In any situation, it's a VID—Very Important Detail—and a priority assignment.

JOBS AND COUNSELING TOO

Not only does the Internet multiply the number of job listings you can find, it also opens the entire area of career help you can receive electronically.

- John Smart (not his real name), a newscaster at a major southwestern TV station, discovered that his contract was not going to be renewed. Frantically, he raced online to a career coach with questions of "WHAT NOW?" John had never heard of outplacement, the process of teaching terminated personnel how to find new employment. The coach he met by computer put him in touch with an outplacement firm in his city. The outplacement consultant helped him understand the customary scope of service offered to people at his level. John was able to negotiate with the TV station for a full outplacement program, which was the only one the station had ever given.

- A college senior in a technical discipline, Karen Krew (pseudonym) lacked related work experience and didn't know how to get started in her chosen career field. Using the same online career coaching firm, Karen found an internship at Apple Computer listed online. After spotting the internship, guest coaches on the online service critiqued Karen's resume and cover letter; other guest coaches gave her interview advice online. It all worked great: Karen landed the internship at Apple.

- Rob Blade (pseudonym) was in the midst of a full outplacement program with a leading nationwide outplacement firm. Rob couldn't bring himself to reveal a career-sensitive problem to his outplacement consultant. His search seemed to be at a standstill. But Rob did go online and reveal his secret to the "anonymous" electronic career coach: Rob has a conviction record. The coach finally convinced Rob the outplacement consultant's viewpoint would be non-judgmental and Rob then felt free to be open about his background. At last news, the job search was back on track.

These three real cases are from the files of Peggy Foster, president of CareerCoach Online (20 Sunnyside Ave., Suite 343A, Mill Valley, CA 94941; Telephone (415) 383-4813; E-mail: info@coach.com).

Foster who until recently was vice president of human resources for Sony Pictures Entertainment, offers advice, support and resources for job search, on-job issues, and entrepreneuring for a small start-up cost, followed by modest monthly charges.

In another example of online counseling, Douglas Sherman, director of career services at Fitchburg State College, offers counseling in the Job-complex area of Delphi (a commercial online information service; call (800) 695-4005 for membership information) one evening a week.

The two make a nice contrast in approach—Foster is focused on "in the trenches" workplace advice, while Sherman's orientation is more academically structured.

Most commercial online services offer counseling services and new ones are springing up on the Internet, manned in many cases by college campus career services professionals. Some services offer counseling or consulting only, but others team advice with job and resume listings. Job-Web, the service of the National Association of Colleges and Employers is an example of a comprehensive resource.

The capacity to go online is updating the entire function of giving career advice. Whether you want counseling or coaching, soon you'll be able to choose from a veritable electronic career carousel.

ONLINE INFORMATION SERVICES

We've used the term "online" frequently in earlier chapters. It merely means a computer is hooked by telephone to giant silos of data. Your own computer, with incredible speed and accuracy, can descend into the silo you've selected and home in on exactly the kernel of knowledge you've asked for. Within seconds, it will be readable on your computer screen.

When you are online, your computer is linked to another computer and the machines are having a chat.

Classified help-wanted ads and other employment information often are transmitted over "online information services," which resemble cable television's programming services of news, comedy, music, talk, movies, and so forth. Unlike cable, which requires a monthly fee, most online services are pay-as-you-go after the initial sign-up fee. Most commercial online information services have, full Internet Access. Much, much more in the way of job resources is available on the full Internet, of course, than on any single commercial online information service.

You choose from a whole menu of categories when you use online information services. Employment is only one category. But for you, the job hunter, it's by far the most important! Here's why:

- Through online information services, you receive data about job openings offered by electronic job ad companies and nonprofit organizations.
- Through online information services, you reach various employment-related databases and informal employment bulletin boards provided by the online information services to their subscribers.
- As an alternative to using online information services, you can gain direct access to stand-alone job services.

If you live in a metropolitan area, you may be able to call online services free or at very low cost because many of them have either local telephone numbers or toll-free 800 numbers.

Whatever the telephone charges to access an online job service, you will need to find the correct telephone number and, in some cases, obtain a password.

Membership in commercial online information services generally isn't free. You can't just call up and plug in. But you can join for a small monthly subscription fee. The amount of the fee varies from service to service and changes from time to time.

Information coverage and prices differ enough to make it worth your time to comparison shop.

The big online services probably offer a larger platter of information than you'll use, and the sheer volume can be confusing. The small services usually are easier to use and less expensive, but may not have everything you need.

In addition to a nominal monthly subscription fee (usually billed automatically to your credit card), many online information services charge for each minute you spend "connected" online in certain categories. (Some categories are billed by the "connected" minute; others are free no matter how long you are connected.)

In addition to the monthly fee and possible connection charges, you have to pay telecommunications charges. There will be no telephone line charges to local access numbers or to 800 numbers (if you pay a flat telephone rate).

If you can't call on a local or an 800 telephone access number, you'll have to pay per-minute toll or long-distance telecommunications charges to the nearest access number. Long-distance telecommunications charges are only 25 cents or less per minute during day hours, and 13 cents or less during night hours.

You may or may not have to pay a modest fee for an online service's start-up kit. As we pointed out earlier, often the start-up kit is included as a bonus item in the purchase of telecommunications hardware such as a modem. Some online services charge for the start-up kit but throw in the first month's subscription fee as part of the package.

Costs can vary widely. Call any service in which you are interested, and obtain a description of the information covered, literature, costs, and, if available, a demonstration of the software.

To recap: The costs of using an online information service to hunt for job openings fall into four possible areas:

1. A monthly subscription fee. (Call the service to determine cost; it may be free.)

2. A connection charge for each minute you are online to specific categories. (Remember, many categories of data are free.)

3. A telecommunications charge. (Usually the cost is only 25 cents or less per minute; it may be free.)

4. A software start-up kit fee. (Usually the kit is inexpensive; often, it's free.)

For a complete listing of online information services, ask at your library for the *Gale Directory of Databases, Volume 1*. This excellent library reference book offers unparalleled scope and depth; there simply isn't a comparable resource available.

Here are some of the larger online information services we've found to have useful employment categories.

▶ **America Online:**   America Online, Inc.
8619 Westwood Center Drive
Vienna, VA 22182
Telephone (800) 827-6364
Fax (703) 556-3750

America Online has been an active online company in career offerings. Among the many resources offered are career articles, the World-Wide Talent Bank (a resume database), cover letter library, self-employment service and the federal employment service.

Still others include an employment agency database, employer contacts database, a jobs listing database and various career guidance services offered by online veteran career counselor James Gonyea.

▶ **CompuServe:**   CompuServe Incorporated
5000 Arlington Centre Boulevard
P.O. Box 20212
Columbus, OH 43220
Telephone (800) 848-8199
Fax (614) 457-0348

CompuServe provides a wide range of moderately priced databases including some that are likely to be useful in a job search.

Like other online services, CompuServe provides several news databases, such as Reuters, Associated Press, Business Wire, and *The Washington Post*. Full-text newspaper coverage is limited compared to other services. For company data, CompuServe's available databases include Value Line financial statements, Standard & Poor's company information, and Investext investment analyst research reports. A host of special interest forums offer ongoing opportunities to network a particular subject; you might, for instance, find out about an engineering position by networking with other engineers.

Members of CompuServe Information Service can search for jobs in CompuServe's classifieds area. The modest monthly fee gives you unlimited connect-time access to 36 basic services, one of which is classifieds. The ads are provided by E-Span, a major job ad service described below.

▶ **Dialog:**   Dialog Information Services
3460 Hillview Avenue
Palo Alto, CA 94304
Telephone (800) 334-2564
Fax (415) 858-7069

This online information service offers more than 400 databases with broad subject coverage, such as agriculture, biology, biotechnology, business and corporate news, chemistry, computers, drugs, economics, energy/environment, engineering, government, humanities, law, medicine, patents and trademarks, science and technology, social sciences, and general reference.

For literature searches, Dialog has abstracts of more than 50,000 journals with at least 2,500 journals, newsletters, and magazines in full text online, as well as 150 newspapers. A few examples: *Los Angeles Times, Boston Globe, USA Today,* and *Business Wire* databases contain full-text coverage.

Other categories, such as the National Newspaper Index, the Legal Resource Index, and the Computer Database, contain abstract information. Executive biographies are available from Marquis Who's Who. Query the company for details of useful data.

▶ **GEnie:**   General Electric Network for Information Exchange
401 North Washington Street
Rockville, MD 20850
Telephone (800) 638-9636

Despite the word "network" in the company name, this is an online information service. It carries a number of useful features that will interest job seekers and career managers.

E-Span, the job ad online service discussed later in this chapter, can be accessed on GEnie.

GEnie carries other services described elsewhere in this book, including the Business Resource Directory (Chapter 5), and Dr. Job and the Home Office/Small Business RoundTable (both in Chapter 7).

▶ **Prodigy:**   Prodigy Services Company
445 Hamilton Avenue,
White Plains, NY 10601
Telephone (800) PRODIGY

This moderately priced service provides access to online classifieds and a careers bulletin board.

The careers bulletin board is not a job listing but a way to electronically do "informational interviewing": you ask people in the job field you're investigating to comment and offer referrals. Members can leave messages about occupations they're considering entering and ask that other members already in that occupation get back to them.

Microsoft Network's Mainstream Career Center

How it benefits you: Here's a one-stop online resource for job searching and career management.

Unlike other online information services which assign in-house staffers to program their content, the Microsoft Network functions like a pipeline through which services of contractors flow.

The Mainstream Career Center is like a big candy shop for job hunters. A job matching system allows you to quickly scan the electronic horizon and see which positions look good. That's for openers—there's much more. Some Mainstream Career Center information content providers (subcontractors) vend information and databases that formerly took hours of hacking your way through the tall weeds of library paperwork.

One subcontractor, Cognetics, provides information about gazelles—the hot companies with lots of jobs. Gale Research's Discovering Jobs and Careers is a gigantic database that profiles comprehensive information for vast numbers of career research projects—from high school investigations to midlife career changes. American Business Information Systems offers data about who's who in companies, and CorpTech shares the scoop on high-tech companies.

Still another vendor will field a computerized method of identifying new occupations for which your transferable skills may qualify you. A variety of testing instruments will appeal to those who need decision-making assistance. Most services are available for a fee, but some are for free, including online networking discussion groups and seminars, as well as tips on resume writing and interviewing.

The Mainstream Career Center (which did not yet have an online address at press time) is operated by a Seattle outplacement firm: Mainstream Access, 4030 Lake Washington Boulevard N.E., Suite 303, Kirkland, WA 98033; E-mail: workplace@msn.com; Telephone (206) 822-6262.

FirePower on the Microsoft Network

This free service is designed specifically for people facing possible job loss through downsizings, early retirement and layoff programs, or—yes!—even being fired. FirePower Career Forum provides real answers to emergency questions: "Where do I go if I want to talk to an attorney?" . . . " What if I have to negotiate?" and much more. With additional online facilities as backup for answers on tough questions about nightmare interview situations, FirePower Career Forum also provides useful exercises, strategies, tips, resume and job posting information for career turbulence. Internet: firepower_msn@msn.com.

ONLINE JOB AD COMPANIES

As we mentioned earlier, individual online job ad services are carried on the general online information services.

In addition, you can find online jobs on the Internet or on electronic job bulletin boards. The ads are presented by:

1. Companies specializing in electronic job ads.
2. Government agencies.
3. Professional societies and trade associations.
4. Industry publications.
5. Job services firms (recruiting agencies).
6. Ad hoc organizations operating as a public service.

Most services displaying electronic help-wanted ads deal with a wide assortment of occupations, or at least a wide assortment in a given career field. But some online job listings are narrowly restricted to certain occupations. For the restricted listings, you will need to be a member of a professional society or trade organization before you can use its job bulletin board.

An example of occupation-specific services is OT Source, an online service for occupational therapists, operated by the American Occupational Therapy Association (1383 Piccard Drive, Rockville, MD 20850; (800) 377-8555) or (301) 948-9626).

OT Source offers many topics of interest to occupational therapists, from new technology to regulatory actions. The one we're interested in is the Job Bank, which lists hundreds of occupational therapy related job openings across the nation. American Occupational Therapy Association members who use the online service pay a modest yearly charge; nonmembers also can subscribe but it costs them more.

Another example is the occupation-specific job bulletin board operated by the Society for Technical Communication (901 North Stuart Street, Suite 904, Arlington, VA 22203; (703) 522-4114).

The bulletin board usually holds some 75 openings for jobs ranging from technical writers to managers. Unless the Society for Technical Communication hears that a position is filled, the listing stays online for two months. Some local chapters maintain bulletin boards of technical jobs in their areas.

Scores of online services are in operation and more are on the way. What follows is a group of services illustrating those that specialize in job ads, also called help-wanted ads, recruitment ads, job listings, or job postings. (Purists find differences in these terms, but most people use them interchangeably.)

▶ **Access . . . FCO On-Line:**   Federal Research Service, Inc.
243 Church Street N.W.
Vienna, VA 22180
Telephone (703) 281-0200
Fax (703) 281-7639

Access is an online service of Federal Research Service, Inc., publishers of a print publication of federal career employment announcements (job openings). The listing contains jobs in Uncle Sam's government. The service is updated every weekday with new job listings.

Available 24 hours a day, this service offers one of the most efficient ways to get current information on federal job openings. You pay an initial set-up fee plus an hourly connect charge. Your account remains active for one year from the date of your last order. Technical staff is available to answer questions about using this service.

You can search by many criteria, such as job level, agency, location, or occupational specialty.

Users in most locations outside the Washington, DC, area can enter the system locally, avoiding long-distance charges.

▶ **America's Job Bank:**   U.S. Department of Labor
(Managed by the New York State Department of Labor, Albany, New York)
Internet World Wide Web address:
http://www.ajb.dni.us

This impressive service is pumping 100,000 job openings a day through a system that can be accessed by home computers around the clock. When fully operational, a million job listings a day will flow through computer screens on Internet, the global network. The jobs—both in private and public sectors—are drawn from public employment service job banks all

Finding and Choosing Online Job Ad Services

Library reference directories aren't the only places where you can chase after job bulletin boards. Try these approaches:

- Call any professional society to which you belong. If the society doesn't have an online job ad service, perhaps the time is ripe to start one.
- Ask at your college's career center and alumni office.
- Page through professional and trade publications, as well as computer magazines such as Computer Shopper, a monthly sold nationwide on newsstands; it contains references to various bulletin boards.

Some local free publications, such as San Diego's Computer-Edge, list bulletin boards, most of which have nothing to do with jobs but you never know when one will turn up.

Another free publication, Computer Currents, lists bulletin boards and is available in a number of large cities. Computer stores usually have copies in racks and you can just pick them up.

One of the problems with a bulletin board system (BBS) run by volunteers is the upkeep. It may become too much of a chore and the BBS goes dead or at least gets very tired.

You want a job BBS that's continually updated and used by enthusiastic, dedicated people. Look for current dates on the screen and notice how many new postings were made since the last time you logged in. A telephone busy signal when you try to get into the job bulletin board isn't a benchmark: It may mean the system is popular because it's good, or it may indicate the bulletin board has a system malfunction.

When accessing an online service, unless otherwise instructed, set your modem software to "8 data bits," "No parity," and "1 stop bit." Then dial your number.

over the country. They range across the occupational spectrum, from secretaries to paralegals, from shipping clerks to managers, and from retail clerks to mechanical engineers.

Traditionally, the public job service offices tended to inventory jobs at the lower end of the status and pay scale. Early feedback suggests this is changing—more upper-level jobs are being added—as employers become aware of the technology that permits them to list job vacancies without cost.

Getting around America's Job Bank is easy on the World Wide Web— you "point and click" on icons and highlighted text. This allows you to view colorful graphics intermingled with the text information.

You don't have to look through the entire 100,000 job database to find what you want. America's Job Bank has a "search engine," which means you indicate the occupation of interest to you, such as "civil engineer," and only the job openings for civil engineers will pop to your screen; all the other tens of thousands of job listings will remain in the database.

America's Job Bank is one more of the several mega services that has the potential to revolutionize job search in this country. (For more

---

Abbreviations Often Used in Online Job Ads

AA	Affirmative action
BA	Bachelor of arts degree
BS	Bachelor of science degree
BSBA	Bachelor of science in business administration
CNE	Certified network engineer
CPA	Certified public accountant
DOD	Department of Defense
DOE	Department of Energy
EOE	Equal opportunity employer
MBA	Master of business administration degree
MS	Master of science degree
M/F/D/V	Male/female/disabled/veteran

Courtesy of E-Span JobSearch

information on this topic, please refer to my book, *Hook Up, Get Hired!*
The Internet Job Search Revolution.)

▶ **Classifacts:**   North American Classifacts
2821 S. Parker Road
Suite 305
Aurora, CO 80014
Telephone (800) 757-7579
Fax (303) 745-1122
Internet: http://www.classifacts.com

This service is a national database of newspaper classified ads and display ads, supplied quickly and directly by the newspapers themselves.

Classifacts allows job seekers to pick up the telephone and instantly
obtain classified ads from almost any major U.S. newspaper market. Approximately 60 newspapers are reported to have signed to supply their
ads to Classifacts. Among the classified offerings in this giant marketplace, consumers will find everything from automobiles to real estate. Job
seekers will select help-wanted ads related to specific occupations or geographic areas.

The process begins when job seekers call the Classifacts number to
buy four-week subscriptions to job ads in their occupational area of interest. They can select ads placed anywhere in the country.

Speedy computers search all the ads from all the newspapers and
report those of interest to the job seekers. A timely printout of the ads is
delivered by surface mail, overnight mail, fax, or modem, and follow-up
reports are delivered for three additional weeks. You could say, for instance, "I want to see everything for dental hygienists in Los Angeles, or
in the New England states."

Classifacts may prove to be among the most valuable tools for long-
distance job hunts, because you don't have to subscribe to a dozen newspapers. The newspapers are participating in electronic pooling of their
classified ads, so you have a reasonable chance to contact employers before the ads become stale and the job openings they describe are filled.

▶ **E-Span:**   8440 Woodfield Crossing
Suite 170
Indianapolis, IN 46240
Telephone (800) 682-2901 or (317) 469-4535
Fax (317) 469-4508

E-Span is one of the nation's largest providers of employment advertising
delivered to personal home computers over the Internet and online information services.

If you sign up, you'll be joining subscribers who have the opportunity to peruse 3,500 listed job openings. These subscribers are reportedly college-educated, computer-literate, professional, managerial, and technically proficient.

For this cream of the crop, the hopeful winds of career advancement are said to be blowing—now, or when the right job comes along.

By tapping into E-Span through one of the online job ad companies' carriers, such as CompuServe or Prodigy, you can browse job opportunities advertised by hundreds of Fortune 1000 companies. You select from more than two dozen categories and then narrow your search by geographic location.

Job listings are available for specific regions of the United States, as well as for Canada and countries throughout the world. The E-Span databases are updated weekly, and advertisements generally run for two weeks.

When you spot a job you think has your name on it, you contact the employer directly, sending your resume via postal mail, e-mail, or fax. Or, if the advertisement so directs, you contact the employer by telephone.

E-Span advertisers have the option of providing a corporate profile along with their job listings. The advertisers contract directly with E-Span to display job openings.

E-Span is an extension of newspaper help-wanted ads. An advertiser places a print help-wanted ad with a newspaper; the newspaper not only prints the ad but, as a value-added service, contracts with E-Span to carry the ad electronically. Advertisers like the combination package because it more widely circulates their recruitment message.

Job seekers should look through E-Span services. (E-Span also operates a resume service, the Candidate Database, but its chief effort is in job openings.) The company maintains an attractive world wide web site on the Internet (http:llwww.espan.com).

▶ **Federal Job Opportunities Board:**   Office of Personnel Management,
Staffing Service Center
4685 Log Cabin Drive
Macon, GA 31298
FJOB Modem (912) 757-3100

"All of Uncle Sam's jobs in one place"—that's a quick description of this government bulletin board service. It includes both current job openings and expected future job openings, labeled as "opportunities."

Once you dial into the system with your PC/modem/communications software, you're told what to do next. The Federal Job Opportunities Board operates like most other online information services. It runs on what is termed a "menu driven" format, which merely means it's step-by-step; if you can read, you can do it.

You will be asked to provide some basic personal information to qualify as a "registered user."

The database is updated every night, which makes it one of the freshest information sources around. Using a job series number or job title, you can search the entire database of every federal job opening and potential job opening for specific positions. You have the option of specifying the government grade level and the state in which the job is located.

The job series number is the number assigned by the federal government to each occupation. When you are in the system, you can activate the help feature and see all the occupations and their corresponding numbers. It's not difficult to use.

If you are not familiar with the job series numbering system, you can search by job title. For instance, if you want to look in the law enforcement area, you might key in the word *law* or *officer*.

For computer specialist, computer programmer, or computer analyst, you might key in the word *compute*. Jobs under all these occupational categories will flash on your screen.

The Federal Job Opportunities Board doesn't stop with job listings. It also issues bulletins that explain the role of the Office of Personnel Management in helping you find your way through the maze of federal employment. The service also details federal salary tables.

An alternative to searching nationwide for federal jobs is to confine your hunt to a particular state. You may prefer to access the Regional Office of Personnel Management Bulletin Boards. You won't get as much information, but you'll spend less money on telephone bills—and some calls won't even be long-distance. The offices usually are closed on weekends.

Here is a list of Regional Office of Personnel Management Bulletin Boards and their telephone numbers:

Atlanta Bulletin Board/Voice	(404)331-3459
Atlanta Bulletin Board/Modem	(404)730-2370
Dallas Bulletin Board/Voice	(214)767-8245
Dallas Bulletin Board/Modem (1200/2400 BPS)	(214)767-0565
Dallas Bulletin Board/Modem (9600 BPS)	(214)767-5471
Detroit Bulletin Board/Voice	(313)226-6950
Detroit Bulletin Board/Modem (2400 BPS)	(313)226-4423
Philadelphia Bulletin Board/Modem (1200/2400 BPS)	(215)580-2216
Philadelphia Bulletin Board/Modem	(201)645-3887

Federal job information is also available at public employment service offices through the Federal Employment Data Services System. You do not operate this system but request a public employment service employee to assist you.

A related and very impressive system you do operate yourself is the Federal Job Information Touchscreen Computer System. It's found at college career centers and job fairs, as well as at public employment service offices.

You just walk right up and touch color blocks on the computer's screen to select the information you want. The system answers back with key points highlighted by the computer's synthetic voice component. If you want the information immediately printed out, all you have to do is finger another block on the screen.

You can search for jobs by state or nationwide, and enter your name and address on the touchscreen to request application forms and materials.

The system gives you a variety of information on federal employment, including announcements about current federal career opportunities, how the hiring process works, and federal jobs for which you may qualify. No moss grows on the touchscreen system—like the Federal Job Opportunities Board and the Federal Employment Data Services System, it's changed daily.

▶ **Jobtrac:**   6856 Arboreal Drive
Dallas, TX 75231
No voice telephone; Modem (214) 349-0527

This electronic job bulletin board is operated by volunteers out of the goodness of their hearts and is free to users. A small contribution is welcome and will be used to update the equipment. The jobs listed range across the board and, although more concentrated in the Greater Dallas-Fort Worth area, can be located anywhere in the nation.

There's quite a story behind this job bulletin board. When Braniff Airlines went into a financial tailspin in 1985, Kerry Goodwin took action. Goodwin, who was president of the Dallas Alliance of Business, asked H. Ross Perot if several programmers at his Electronic Data Systems company could assist in creating software for a bulletin board system to help 3,000 of the airline's employees find new jobs. It worked! That service, Jobtrac, continues to this day, operated by a half-dozen selfless volunteers, still quarterbacked by Kerry Goodwin.

It banners jobs in a spectrum of occupational fields: accounting, administrative, education, engineering, medical, nonprofit, professional, sales, secretarial, and technical careers.

There's more. Jobtrac gives you federal employment opportunities in the state of Texas and identifies about two dozen nationwide job bulletin boards.

Goodwin says, "We accept jobs from anywhere that people want to list." Job seekers can contact employers directly (best way) or modem back their resumes.

Jobtrac offers information on job search topics ranging from writing resumes to applying for federal jobs. This is a real public service and you should remember to say "Thank you."

▶ **JobTrak:**   1990 Westwood Boulevard
Suite 260
Los Angeles, CA 90025
Telephone (800) 999-8725
Fax (310) 475-7912
Internet: http://www.jobtrak.com

One of the hottest job listing services to hit the Internet is the JobTrak Internet Network. This database is publishing more than 550 new job listings a day from employers seeking to hire college students and graduates. In addition to the job listings, more than 500 in-depth company profiles are accessible through the network. Unlike most of the job listing databases on the Net, JobTrak allows employers to target their advertising.

For college students and recent graduates, JobTrak is an outstanding source of information about job openings, employer profiles, job hunting tips and employment statistics. "The days of sorting through binders of job listings are over," say grateful students. As one explains: "Using my computer I can tap into JobTrak and search for a job or research a company."

JobTrak says it is used by more than 150,000 small and large employers to fill part- and full-time openings. Says a leading recruitment manager: "Throughout the year we'll use JobTrak to help fill a variety of positions. We find it's very useful for attracting both students seeking entry level jobs and experience people who may be attending graduate school as part of their own career advancement plan."

The company has unique relationships with college career centers across the nation. "College campuses have traditionally been a source for employers to recruit high quality employees," says Connie Ramberg, Job-Trak founder. "By partnering with the career centers and posting the job listings online, we've increased the employers' exposure to students and alumni, more than 300 career centers across the nation now partner with JobTrak. These campuses include UCLA, Stanford, Columbia, Georgia

Tech, Purdue, George Washington, USC, Virginia Tech, and Duke, to name a few."

▶ **LA Online:**   332 Hermosa Avenue
Suite 7
Hermosa Beach, CA 90254
Telephone (310) 372-9364
Modem (310) 372-4050

LA Online is an online database serving Los Angeles. Along with shopping, news, and regular features, it includes two sections useful to job seekers.

The first gives users access to the classified help-wanted ads from Los Angeles' largest community publications.

You simply type "Go News," select the publication of your choice, and pull up the classified listing in each newspaper.

On-line Career Fair is the second selection job seekers can choose. These are job listings not taken from newspapers but directly posted to the LA Online. The size of On-line Career Fair goes up and down with the job climate. At times, only a dozen or so jobs are posted; at other times, thousands of jobs are noted.

Access to LA Online is free.

▶ **Networking Careers On-Line:**   Network World Bulletin Board System
161 Worcester Road
Framingham, MA 01701
Telephone (800) 622-1108
Fax (508) 879-3167
Modem (up to 2400 BPS) (508) 620-1160
Modem (up to 9600 BPS) (508) 620-1178

Computer and computer networking specialists make between 4,000 and 6,000 calls monthly to this service, which mirrors the job ads in *Network World* magazine. Except for telephone charges, the online job ad service is free to job seekers.

The job bulletin board carries a full month's worth of ads from the magazine, plus information about companies' corporate backgrounds. By using the bulletin board, you can get a head start on magazine readers because the jobs are posted electronically on Friday and printed the following Monday.

Networking Careers On-Line accepts resumes electronically and faxes them to employers. Other service features include a career forum where participants share information and advice about career opportunities and employment-related subjects.

NEWSPAPER ONLINE INFORMATION SERVICES

Being newspaper people, we're popping our buttons to tell you that a number of North America's great papers are doing their share to bring you a world of information at prices that won't flatten your wallet.

Major newspaper companies are working together to find the best ways to deliver the news electronically. The Media Laboratory at Massachusetts Institute of Technology is conducting research for a consortium of newspapers, as well as for computer maker International Business Machines Corporation. This could lead to dramatic changes; already, newspapers are moving beyond the printed page through computer networks and telephone lines.

Newspapers were early pioneers in electronic services in the 1980s. The timing must not have been right because, in the main, they lost millions of dollars. Some call that era the newspaper industry's "Vietnam."

The deep hit in the pockets that newspapers took on early consumer electronic services left them shell-shocked. But now, according to reports from the Newspaper Association of America's Randy Bennett, interest appears to be growing in online services to supplement—not replace—the printed word.

The *Fort Worth Star-Telegram* is the industry standard-bearer for the longest, and generally profitable, operation of its online service, StarText.

Launched in 1982, StarText has undergone several reincarnations. Subscribers today can have an information picnic on StarText at a small charge per month for unlimited use.

Of the many StarText features, the number one and number two choices for job campaigners are the opportunities to get an early look at help-wanted ads, available the evening prior to publication, and to review the current business news, available in depth for the previous seven days.

The smorgasbord of non-job-related StarText features includes local news, features, travel services, entertainment, message boards, reference services, sports, an encyclopedia, stock and mutual fund prices, and more.

The *St. Louis Post-Dispatch* uses the *Star-Telegram* software for its system, PostLink. Beyond classified ads, available the previous evening, and the full local news report, PostLink offers an electronic bazaar of leisure-time and lifestyle features, including four hours on a national on-line service for a modest fee.

Access Atlanta, the service of the *Atlanta Journal and Constitution,* charges a small monthly fee for unlimited access to many features, including the classified ads.

An attractive feature of Access Atlanta is the "search" function. You avoid hours of searching for specific information merely by telling your computer the appropriate keywords, such as *environmental* or *sales.* The computer does the rest, zapping onto your screen every shred of data related to the keywords you select.

Chicago Online is produced by the Tribune Company, owner of the *Chicago Tribune.* The contents of the *Chicago Tribune* are made available online daily. Using keywords, you can search not only the service's extensive classified job listings, but the entire paper.

Beyond the newspaper online, Chicago Online offers a wide array of information, forums, and message boards for and about the Chicagoland area, all for a tiny basic cost per month.

A joint venture between the Tribune Company and America Online (described elsewhere in this chapter), the service is considered a "local area" of America Online. You get access to the full service of America Online when you subscribe to Chicago Online and vice versa.

In Canada, the evolution of online services can be followed by observing the changes in CompuSpec, the electronic system of The Hamilton Spectator. Initiated in 1986, the early features included some with news content, but the most popular offering has been the classified help-wanted ads.

In 1991, the ability to send electronic letters to the editor and a few interactive teleconferences (groups of people electronically chatting with each other) were added.

In 1993, the SPEC (Spectator Public Electronic Community) Link was launched. More than 30 new forums (special interest groups) were created to cover a wide range of topics from social issues to local economy concerns. The SPEC Link is a kind of community clue. Chiming in are business leaders, newspaper writers, patrons of public libraries, people with disabilities, and senior citizens, among thousands of other area residents.

Employment-related teleconferencing has proven to be of enduring interest. Discussions range from shared experiences of adult job seekers to students who talk about finding summer jobs.

The Hamilton Spectator gives this rationale for mounting a serious electronic effort: "We want to maintain our position as our community's information hub. Building a strong new network of people communicating with each other is good for newspapers and the communities they serve."

Mercury Center, an experiment of the *San Jose (California) Mercury News* is a fully searchable online service that includes help-wanted ads and access to all of the newspaper's stories since 1985, among other features. It was a new venture as this book was written.

Still more newspapers are operating some type of online service. Try the sources listed on page 119 for starters.

A business and library reference, *Newspapers Online,* published by BiblioData (P.O. Box 61, Needham Heights, MA 02194; 617-444-1154) is the directory that keeps track of more than 150 local, regional, national, and international daily newspapers that are online in full text. Classified ads usually are not included.

When you want to research company news, industry facts, or occupational information in more than one newspaper, particularly papers in a distant location, explore the use of online services that store newspapers. More than 100 newspapers worldwide offer access to their electronic libraries (files of stories—but not the classified ads—that have appeared in the newspaper over several years) through DataTimes, 14000 Quail Springs Parkway, Suite 450, Oklahoma City, OK 73134; (800) 642-2525. Look for this comprehensive service at large libraries or through independent information professionals.

DIALOG (described elsewhere in this chapter) also offers more than 50 newspapers' electronic libraries.

How can you use the rich resources in these newspapers? *Newspapers Online* editor Susanne Bjorner explains: "Suppose you are interested in finding a job in a particular geographic area, or in a particular industry. By doing a 'global' [all-encompassing] search in many newspapers at one time you can pull up lists of places to try.

"Our directory helps searchers know which sections of each newspaper would provide likely hunting grounds, and what they're called— business, money, metro, city, front page, and so on," Bjorner says.

Learning to use a wealth of newspapers vastly increases your career mobility, a key element in making sure your career remains on an upward track.

The electronic neighborhood is a reality in every community, observes John Granatino, director of electronic publishing at the *Providence (R.I.) Journal-Bulletin,* another newspaper now thinking electronic thoughts.

"As the rising percentage of household modem ownership and growing membership in national online services attest, more and more adults are going electronic to satisfy their needs for immediate information and immediate interaction with other people," Granatino says.

This includes individuals who are looking for new jobs immediately or who want to keep their antenna up for ongoing opportunity.

Prediction: Despite the heavy financial losses in electronic ventures during the 1980s, newspapers increasingly are seeing themselves as being in the business of communications rather than in the business of newspapers. Newspapers will become more important, not less important, in your job search.

THOUGHTS ON USING ONLINE HELP-WANTED ADS

Some estimates place the percentage of job openings that employers do *not* advertise at between 60 percent and 80 percent.

Even so, recruitment advertising is the single best source of identifying employers who have immediate job openings. The key reasons are described in the following sections.

More Job Advertising May Be Generated

"That single best source can get even better," says a recruiter in the Midwest. Why? "Money," answers the recruiter.

"You need people to prepare the ads, screen the replies, and send back letters of acknowledgment or regret—all that before other people even evaluate the real candidates. Electronics has become the magic wand of instant action. You can recruit with fewer people.

"Once the word about the new applicant tracking systems [described in the last chapter] trickles down, employers may be more willing to advertise their openings through both print and electronic media," the recruiter explains.

Job Ads Offer Immediate Employment

When it comes to putting rocket boosters under your job search campaign, print or electronic help-wanted ads are far superior to searching out jobs through slower-developing opportunities such as networks, employee referrals, walk-ins, public and private job services, and job fairs.

Despite the folklore we've all heard about phony help-wanted advertising designed merely to check the labor market—to see whether a current employee will reveal "disloyalty" by responding to the ad, or to accomplish a similarly devious design—the fact is the overwhelming majority of help-wanted ads are the real thing. They offer real jobs that are really available—and available *now*. Advertising has become too costly for employers to play games.

To put your efforts into perspective, bear this in mind: print media help-wanted ads remain the dominant recruiting source companies use. Study after study has shown this to be true.

Electronic help-wanted ads are joining print in the recruiting arsenals of employers, and you won't want to miss out on opportunities in an economy that is rapidly changing from one of a lot of hard-working people to one where there are fewer, smart-working people.

Old Ads Can Yield New Leads

Studying history can be a clue to the future. This is a theory job seekers use in looking back at old print classified help-wanted ads. By looking back eight to ten weeks, you might find a job not yet filled or one in which a false start was made by a new hire no longer with the company.

By looking back a year or two, you might discover a position from which the person hired has advanced or moved on, leaving a similar position open now. A downside to electronic job ads is usually that you can't look back. Most ads are deleted on a timely basis.

When you find an exception, an old electronic ad in your field, the same principle applies as for print ads: You've identified an employer who hires your kind of talent. Seize the initiative and apply.

MAKE ONLINE JOB ADS WORK FOR YOU

Match Replies and Requests

Once you find an electronic job listing to which you'd like to respond, study its wording and the priority of requirements. Work hard to make your cover letter and resume directly reflect the ad—yes, use the same keywords and synonyms for those keywords.

As a creative writing major says after "going electronic" in her job search, "Electronically speaking, I have learned not to be too clever. If they ask for 'excellent communication and interpersonal skills,' I tell them I have 'excellent communication and interpersonal skills.' I never knew how nice repetition could sound," she says with a grin.

Focus only on specific experiences sought by the employer, or on achievements you want to stand out. As much as possible, match each job requirement with a qualification you offer—documented by specific achievements.

Think in terms of key descriptors—college, major, grade point average, engineering specialty, language fluency, years of experience, and the like. Stress your accomplishments.

Avoid lumbering on with a laundry list of duties and responsibilities unrelated to the job at hand. (How to market your qualifications and respond to electronic job ads is discussed more fully in our companion book, *Electronic Resume Revolution.*)

Read between the Lines

Some people assume if something is new or technical, it must be right. In evaluating job listings on an electronic delivery system, it's best not to take anything at face value just because the information is coming to you in an unfamiliar format.

Just as you emphasize your strengths in a resume, advertisers stress their strong points in attracting your attention, whether by print or online delivery. They'd be fools not to showboat their positives.

An advertisement that emphasizes an "attractive plant" may mean the facilities are exceptionally pleasant, or it may be designed to distract your attention from the job's low pay.

An ad that highlights "excellent salary and benefits" may mean the employer is willing to pay for quality, or it may be deceptive in that it fails to include the fact that you're expected to put in 50-hour workweeks to receive great pay.

A larger than usual ad may suggest that the employer places a great degree of importance on the position, or that the employer runs a marginal workplace and needs to keep replacing people who leave.

Your hope is that what you see in an ad is what you get. The plant is gorgeous. The salary is superb. The employer appreciates good people.

You may get clues about the nature of the employer or the company culture from the way an electronic recruitment ad is worded and presented, but you can't be sure about an employer's perspective or agenda until you investigate further.

Stretch Your First Impressions

Don't prematurely assume that you are wrong for a job or that you don't want a job. Apply for anything in the neighborhood of what you want and can do, even if the pay is lower than your market value.

Why apply for a job that pays less than your market value? One reason is employers can't always find a mirror image of the employee they'd like to hire. They might be willing to upgrade a position for a senior person. Similarly, the employer may be willing to add another job for someone with potential but not enough experience.

Negotiate if Possible

Advertised job openings may give an impression that the salary offer is fixed, with no room for negotiation. In highly structured bureaucracies, salary negotiation is an uphill battle. To succeed you usually must get the position upgraded or move up the ladder to a higher position. In less structured settings, you may find employers more flexible than you may first think.

Try Out for Many Hats

Even if the job is not up to your standards, bear in mind what we discovered in the last chapter: *Once you're in a company's database, you can be called out for any job whose requirements match your qualifications— now or next year.*

It's a reasonable guess that companies advanced enough to advertise their job openings electronically probably are sophisticated enough to do applicant tracking electronically.

MORE POINTERS FOR READING ELECTRONIC HELP-WANTED ADS

Answer on First Ring

Respond at once to electronic ads that meet your qualifications. In responding to print help-wanted ads, it's often best to time your response to arrive a day or two after the big crush of mail. In viewing electronic ads, you can't be sure when the ad was first beamed out and you may be viewing it in the last days of its run.

Follow Up

After you respond to online ads, follow up. In addition to sending your resume (via modem, fax, or mail) to the person or address given in the ad, try to find out the name of the hiring manager. Mail or hand-deliver a copy of your resume to that manager, addressed by name and proper title.

Network to find a contact at the company and ask the contact to put in a good word for you with both the employment manager and the hiring manager. Start with electronics, and end with personal touch.

Search Resourcefully

Search large ads for "hidden" personnel requirements. Many big ads seek technical people, but they may be a small part of a company's work force. Ask about other openings to support the advertised jobs.

See through Titles

Thousands of job titles are common in the U.S. job market. One occupation may be known by a spectrum of titles, depending on the industry or the employer. An electrical engineer may be called a design engineer, a sales engineer, a test engineer, or an electronics research engineer—and these are only a few variations. When you're scrolling through the screens, remember a rose is a rose is a rose. Don't hesitate to apply even when you're not positive the job title listed is equivalent to the labels you use to describe the work you're capable of doing.

Manage Blind Ads

Blind ads, those that do not identify the employer, sometimes are used to avoid a huge response that could create a clerical monster. The easy-to-manage software may mean we'll be seeing fewer and fewer blind ads now that companies want resumes and can quickly send out acknowledgment letters.

Blind ads are also run to keep openings quiet, especially for jobs at a senior level.

When you spot an electronic blind ad you're tempted to answer, use caution to make sure your response doesn't wind up on your present employer's desk. Just as newspapers and trade journals offer blocking systems to bar any list of employers you specify from receiving your resume, so do operators of some online recruitment services.

Make sure you understand the confidentiality protection offered by the service you use. Learn exactly what the process offers and follow the instructions precisely.

If you live in fear of your employer's discovering you're restless, and you're not 100 percent certain that your resume is "safe," as a desperate resort you can use the third-person dodge for responding to a plum advertisement.

We don't recommend the third-person screen as something you should ordinarily try. But there are times when it's virtually the only move if you wish to respond to a choice blind ad.

In this stratagem, you ask a friend to respond for you. The friend contacts the employer: "I have an associate who appears to be an extraordinarily perfect match for your job requirements. My associate has asked that I serve as the liaison until mutual identities are established. Please telephone me at the following number and I will be pleased to put you in touch with my associate."

What does your friend say if the person who calls is, horrors, your boss?

Your friend truthfully mumbles that, upon reflection, the associate realizes the job is a mismatch, the salary is inadequate, the vacation requirement is three months, and thanks a lot, Mr. Boss, but no thanks.

Use Ads to Prospect

By staying current with the ads, you'll know which companies are expanding and hiring more personnel. When you see a company in a hiring mode, telephone to learn the name of the hiring manager in the area you'd like to work.

You may have trouble obtaining the appropriate name. Companies are wary about executive recruiters pirating their key personnel, or about job seekers bothering them with calls for employment. Be persistent; if you're quizzed, say it's personal and you're writing a letter, which is true.

Your letter to the hiring manager should outline your qualifications and offer convincing reasons for your wanting to work for the company. Request an appointment to talk about present or future job openings.

If you get in and nothing clicks, ask for referrals to the hiring manager's contacts in other companies.

Studies of how jobs are found show varying results, but it's commonly believed that a bare minimum of 20 percent of all available jobs are advertised. With 5 million jobs filled every year, that's quite a few. Even people who rely on networking as a primary job hunt strategy may miss out by failing to follow job ads.

Use Standard Job Descriptions

When you're thinking about responding to an ad but aren't quite sure you have a solid handle on the position's fine print, refer to a job description that closely matches the position.

Libraries have copies of job description books; a number are in electronic form, such as Job Scribe (see Chapter 7), a database of 3,000 authentic job descriptions from real companies for positions ranging from entry-level hires to senior executives.

Use Job Listings to Advance

Electronic surfing is useful in career management.

Suppose you think you might like to change your line of work but aren't sure what training and credentials you'll need. Recruitment ads to the rescue!

Read all the help-wanted ads, print and electronic. You may see, for instance, that employment calls for travel agents leave no doubt that a familiarity with computerized reservations systems is a must. You'll learn that office staff may be turned away if they do not know specific programs, such as Lotus or WordPerfect. You'll see that drafters must be literate in computer-assisted design.

If you seem to be missing a brick or two in your skills foundation, a crash seminar or a course at a community college or university can quickly build professional strength.

Even when you're not switching fields, you may want to refocus your campaign to fast-forward your job hunt. You may, for instance, find ten listings for entry-level marketers in environmental firms and only two for medical companies. A book on environmental studies can color your language green.

If you have any doubt about the kind of qualifications you need for the next step up the ladder, reading electronic help-wanted ads will be enlightening.

Summing up, the technology of advertising for help has come a long way from an 1870s ad in a frontier newspaper for people to get the mail from one place to another:

> Help Wanted. Pony Express Riders.
> Apply in person. High risk, low pay.
> Orphans preferred.

LIGHTS, CAMERA, JOBS!

If you'd rather watch or listen to recruitment advertising than read help-wanted ads, the telecommunications industry may be able to oblige.

Television and radio stations around the nation are creating programs to help people find work.

Typically, they receive good media reviews. They're novel and newsy and they hit the spot for a generation that grew up on television viewing.

Responding to job ads on television and radio may be free—you answer as though they are print recruitment ads. In some cases, a cost shifting takes place: the job seeker is forced to pay a few dollars to respond to the ad by calling a 900 telephone number.

It may be worth it to you to pay this slight administrative charge to receive a formal application form that will be read by a computer and evaluated against the job requisition.

Unfortunately for legitimate companies that view 900 numbers as profit centers, the shady and sleazy reputation of the early 900-number telephone industry may be a difficult obstacle to overcome in persuading job seekers to place their calls.

According to the Federal Trade Commission (FTC), you should be cautious of employment ads directing applicants to call 900 numbers.

In one paraphrased sample complaint to the Federal Trade Commission, a letter writer says:

> I saw an ad in the newspaper for a construction job. The ad said to dial an 800 toll-free number for an application. When I called, I was told to dial a 900 number to find out about job openings in my area. When I called that number, a recording told me to send a stamped, self-addressed envelope to have a job application mailed to me. All I got was a one-page generic job application and a 900-number charge for $39.00 on my telephone bill.

The FTC recently sued two companies advertising jobs in the United States using 900 numbers. These companies not only failed to disclose the cost of each call, which ranged between $10 and $18, but also they provided little, if any, information that would lead to a job.

Before you spend money to respond to a job ad, know what the 900-number call will cost. Reputable employment service companies will state the costs upfront. If you're ripped off with telephone charges for 900-number calls made to a fraudulent business, contact your telephone company immediately and ask that the charges be deleted.

To learn more, send for the free FTC booklets *Job Hunting: Should You Pay?* and *"900" Numbers.* They're available from the Federal Trade Commission, Public Reference, Washington, DC 20580.

We've alerted you to a *potential* for abuse. A number of classy operations have put in 900-number services. They range from the Consumers Union (the eternal foe of ripoffs) to the Catholic News Service.

"There is nothing inherently tarnished about 900 numbers," says a Consumers Union representative. And that's so. You are merely paying for information ranging from automobile resale values to movie reviews that factor in family values.

Quite apart from 900-number job scams, one more obstacle for 900 numbers as employment facilitators is the fact that applying for work is seen as an entitlement in this country.

Historically, American culture has not required people who are looking for jobs to pay a third-party fee merely to respond to employers who advertise open positions. This is true even when the third party says it is assisting the employer with the added service of "prescreening"—performing a computer match of the job requisition against the job seekers' applications before sending candidates to the employer. The entire cost of recruiting traditionally has fallen on the employer. For most Americans, the idea of paying to apply for work will take some mental reprogramming.

If the 900 pay-per-response idea becomes commonly accepted, the next question is: How will the working poor be able to afford to even look for work if it costs $4 or $5 a pop just to obtain an application?

Most of the jobs that are advertised on television and radio shows and require response through a 900-number system will not be near the lower rungs of the career ladder.

MORE WAYS TO TAP TECHNOLOGY FOR JOB LEADS

As most people realize, the one-company career is all but obsolete. The days of "lifers" are over yesterday's hill.

If you do not want to be left behind yesterday's hill as well, you must know what kinds of jobs to go after and how to look for a new one when conditions change.

An advanced strategy to do this is roaring down the tracks like a great opportunity express. This spectacular new tool is the electronic employer database.

5 Amazing New Electronic Employer Databases

For Dynamite Made-to-Order Job Leads, Nothing Beats These Information Age Tools

The previous chapter took us through electronic resources for recruitment advertising—actual advertised job openings that employers say they want to fill.

The other side of finding prospective employers is tapping into what is called the "hidden job market"—jobs that exist but are not advertised.

Computers can broaden your search arena by producing high-possibility target lists of people who can hire you.

Be honest. Would you turn down these opportunities to customize: A house you designed? A tailor-made suit? A world cruise where you chart the course? Neither would we, and that's what this chapter is about: how you can call the shots.

You have the power to write a wish list to describe your dream employer. You could jot down such criteria as:

- The kind of work you want to do.
- The kind of companies or organizations for which you want to work.
- The size of company you prefer.
- The company's financial stability.
- The location you prefer.

After you design a preferred profile of your next employer, you tell databases to search for these criteria and to print out a list of every potential employer that meets this profile. By using a computer, it's almost as easy as snapping your fingers.

What makes it possible is the 1990s' proliferation of electronic employer databases.

Outplacement and job search consultants have been using electronic databases since the 1980s, as a shortcut to the hidden job market.

But don't most people draw up job lists by using enormous print directories? If you want to struggle for hours to identify potential employers, you can still thumb through print directories, but electronic databases make it possible to quickly cut to the job chase. We're for that, aren't you?

DATABASES CLOSE UP

If you need a thumbnail definition of a database and a databank, here's the classic analogy. A database, a file of information, is like a chapter in a book. A databank is the book itself, consisting of many databases or "chapters."

In one sense, the database industry is at the chicken-or-egg stage of development. Most databases are too expensive to use on home computers, but developers are hesitant to invest huge sums of money to bring the prices down until there's greater demand. In time, there will be better balance; now, only a few databases for job hunters are definitely priced for home use.

Electronic employer databases come in various formats. The three most common are:

1. *Online*—Computer services can be either commercial or college-campus-operated; both types list information about employers. An online database usually is a one-way exchange. But in a few services, it is structured as an interactive system permitting job seekers to ask questions of recruiters and receive answers. It is designed to direct the job seeker in approaching a particular industry or profession.

2. *CD-ROM* (Compact Disk-Read Only Memory)—An informational service can give details similar to those available with the online service, but they are recorded on a compact disk and can be read

Tips for Searching in a Database

Entering the world of information is like traveling to another planet—there's so much that has never been explored. If you've decided to go-it-alone on your research for a new job rather than enlist the help of an information broker, here are a few pointers. Author and information guru Sue Rugge (The Information Broker's Handbook, Windcrest/McGraw-Hill, 1995) has kindly provided us with tips to help smooth out what can be a bumpy road along your job search adventure.

1. Tapping this type of online database requires practice, skill, documentation, and training which, with many vendors, costs additional money, not to mention the sign-up fees at the start. There are thousands of databases on some hundreds of systems.

2. Your job is to get a job, not to become a researcher. There is no question, however, that learning about these resources may help you not only to find a job but to do an even better job when you get one.

3. The online information industry has a lot of weaknesses. If you approach this rich resource area as if it were a mature industry, you're likely to become disappointed, frustrated, and confused. It's still a wild and woolly place, particularly for new users. Keep your eyes open, and, until you feel you know what you're doing, keep your wallet close to your chest.

4. The real Achilles heel for the online information industry is inaccurate information. Most of us used to think that if something is in print, it has to be true. A small typo—a single letter—can be enough to throw off an entire search.
   For example, on one major service, there are 30,000 occurrences of the word "automobile" and another 300 for "automobiel." This is a problem for at

(continued)

Tips for Searching in a Database (cont.)

least two reasons. First, if you are searching for articles on automobiles you will not find the references in which that word is misspelled. Second, if mistakes are made in the text, they can also be made in numerical data where detection is next to impossible.

5. Every database has different access codes even when several are on the same vendor system. You cannot search the databases without a road map—the vendor's "user documentation." Each database on DIALOG has chapters of documentation running between 30 and 50 pages, and each costs to print.

6. Every vendor system has a different language. Although the concepts of searching are the same throughout the industry, the means and commands for employing these concepts differ widely. You will have to learn an entirely different "language" for each online system you wish to search.

   There are things you can do on one system that simply can't be done on others. This is another reason to make sure you've not only selected the right database but are searching it on the most cost-effective system for your needs.

7. Don't always trust the update advisory provided by vendors. The advertised update schedule is not always met.

8. Time is money. Remember that most of these services make their money on your per-minute connect time. Who provides the greatest sources of revenue? Bumbling amateurs, who don't know what they're doing. For this and all the reasons above, a good argument can certainly be made for hiring a professional when you want to tap these powerful and sophisticated resources of information.

> ### Tips for Searching in a Database (cont.)
>
> 9. The above comments apply mainly to the large biblio-graphic and directory systems, but being forewarned will help you when searching the job offerings databases as well.

only by a CD-ROM player attached to a computer. CD-ROM is not interactive and cannot be updated by the user.

Most of the CD-ROM products mentioned in this chapter are also available online.

3. *Computer diskette*—Some database services issue their information on the popular 5¼" or 3½" computer diskettes that nearly all PCs can read. The database service updates information on a periodic basis by simply issuing a new, inexpensive diskette.

TWO WAYS TO USE A DATABASE IN A JOB HUNT

The first way to use an employer database is to construct a target employer list.

The second way is to develop in-depth knowledge about specific companies and their personnel to use in job interviews. It is much easier to show how your qualifications fit a position's requirements when you know about the position and about the company. For the best jobs, *advance research* is essential whether it comes from electronics, print, or people.

Because developing job leads and doing pre-interview research overlap, we discuss them together in this chapter.

Basically, you are trying to find out such things as a firm's marketing methods, growth plans, research and development plans, product development or manufacturing plans, financial stability, employee benefits, quality as an employer, position in the industry, opportunity for advancement, reputation for keeping promises to employees, and so forth.

You want to know the names of the managers and executives, their biographies (maybe you went to the same school), and any hot news that may help you get hired.

Anticipate how helpful it could be if you were prepared to discuss all the business- and trade-press articles written about a company in the two years prior to going in for an interview with one of the company's executives. If you use the material gracefully, without sounding overprepared, such careful attention is impressive!

When you merely ask the computer to create a target list, the computer may identify, for example, 240 small companies and 39 large companies—with full contact information for managers of these companies—that meet the criteria you entered for location, industry, size, and type of organization.

Instead of calling into a bank of company switchboards too formidable to contemplate, you call up a database and ask your questions. In a few minutes—*voila!*—the computer spits out pages of the research needed to mount a first-class job marketing campaign.

If you're fuzzy about where you want to work, doing a customized target search is a waste of time and money. But if you know what you want, an electronic search is precision bombing that hits its target.

Let's look at another example. You can, for instance, establish target parameters and then go into the database and direct it to give you all the companies within a particular field that are located in your preferred geographic area and fit into your company-size boundaries of, say, $20 million to $100 million in annual sales.

Depending on how your search is structured, you'll have tons of information. If you've read other job hunt guides, you know how important it is to keep good records. You can use the sample format in Figure 5–1 for your top 20 or so job leads. Because you are unique and your search is unique, improve on this sample format by adding considerations that are important to you.

TIPS ON USING THE GREAT RESEARCH MACHINE

Using online databases isn't yet cheap, unless you live by the motto "Time is money."

If you're a new convert, you may be able to find a continuing education course or a community college to introduce you to the basics. When you're paying the bill, practice on inexpensive online databases, such as those on Knowledge Index on CompuServe, a service that operates at a discount at night and on weekends. Use free resources available on the Internet when possible.

Organization _____

Address _____ City _____

State _____ Zip _____ Telephone _____ Fax/Modem _____

Key Personnel _____

Company Demographics

    Number of employees _____

    Quality of benefits _____

    Quality as an employer _____

    Opportunity for advancement _____

    Annual gross revenue (sales) _____

    Earnings _____

    Financial stability _____

    Facility locations _____

    Product(s) _____

    New product development _____

    Marketing methods _____

    Potential for expansion _____

    To where _____

Problem areas _____

Planned Personnel _____

    Positions I could fill _____

    Qualifications I have _____

Figure 5–1   Employer Research Data Form

The cost of using the databases on CD-ROM or diskette varies widely. Some career counseling and outplacement firms offer them as part of their services. Many libraries carry employer databases. Some that you can buy for home use cost about the same as other software programs.

How can you identify the databases you want to search? Look through the list in the next section. No matter what your career field, chances are you'll find a database of interest. Don't be overwhelmed by the number of databases—they're enough to scramble anybody's calculator. Read through all the examples and mark those that are of particular interest for further exploration.

EXAMPLES OF ELECTRONIC EMPLOYER DATABASES

▶ **Barterbase:** Trustee Center for Professional Development
Hartwick College
Oneonta, NY 13820
Telephone (607) 431-4425
Fax (607) 431-4008

This is an excellent database of companies that are good targets for liberal arts graduates.

Barterbase is maintained by a consortium of liberal arts colleges to help their graduates in the job search. Hartwick College in Oneonta, New York, took the lead in creating the consortium and serves as coordinator.

Each of the participating colleges contributes to the database. Hartwick College supports a database for private schools with teacher-fellowship programs. Hamilton College maintains a database of law firms that hire paralegals. Oberlin College is responsible for a database of publishers who hire editorial assistants.

Dickinson College's database is filled with international job opportunities. St. Lawrence University concentrates on environmental employers. Colby College lists those who hire in the performing arts and museums.

Students at member colleges can receive a computer disk with the relevant information, or they can turn on a modem-equipped computer, tap into the system, and directly request information online.

Because liberal arts majors often find it tough to land a job, Barterbase serves as a welcome source of information and a way to get to the so-called "hidden job market," including unadvertised jobs with smaller employers.

▶ **Business ASAP on InfoTrac:** Information Access Company
362 Lakeside Drive
Foster City, CA 94404
Telephone (800) 227-8431;
Fax (415) 378-5369

This CD-ROM database contains the complete text of approximately 350 titles indexed in *Business Index, Business & Company Profile,* and *General BusinessFile.*

Subjects covered in this service include business and industry, trade, management, and other business-related topics. Call the toll-free number for pricing information.

▶ **Business & Company ProFile:**   on InfoTrac, Public Edition
Information Access Company
362 Lakeside Drive
Foster City, CA 94404
Telephone (800) 227-8431
Fax (415) 378-5369

Updated monthly, this CD-ROM database is a comprehensive source for business research on companies, products, markets, industries, economics, and management disciplines.

The Business & Company ProFile indexes and abstracts about 700 business, management, and trade journals and links them to directory information for more than 140,000 private and public companies.

This is a job seeker's dream: The service can spit out the full text of the news releases about companies carried on the PR Newswire. If you want to know what a company is proud of, this is a quick way to find out. Business and Company ProFile also contains indexing to four major newspapers.

Another plus: You can keystroke in a city or state and retrieve the top 100 companies in that area, ranked by sales volume. Or you can search by industry or SIC (standard industrial code) to produce a list of companies within that industry, ranked by sales volume. All in all, a service not to miss.

▶ **Business America on CD-ROM:**   American Business Information, Inc.
5711 South 86th Circle
P.O. Box 27347, Omaha, NE 68127
Telephone (402) 593-4565
Fax (402) 331-6681

This ultimate desk-top marketing tool lists more than 10 million U.S. businesses, including retailers, wholesalers, service companies, and professional firms.

The Business America On CD-ROM database includes key names, addresses, telephone numbers, and number of employees, annual sales volume, credit rating codes and more!

▶ **Business Periodicals Index:**   H. W. Wilson Company
950 University Avenue
Bronx, NY 10
Telephone (800) 367-6770
Fax (718) 590-1617

This CD-ROM disk service contains more than 545,000 clips from articles and book reviews in some 345 business periodicals. Business Periodicals Index includes feature articles, interviews, biographical sketches of business leaders, book reviews, research developments, and new product reviews—loads of information for the job seeker wanting to do serious research on an industry or specific companies within an industry.

Some of the areas of business covered in this service include: accounting, advertising, banking, building and construction, chemical industry, communications, computers, economics, electronics, engineering, finance, food industry, government regulations, industrial relations, insurance, international business and management, marketing, and personnel administration.

Nuclear energy, occupational health and safety, oil and gas, public relations, publishing, real estate, and regulations of industry and transportation are also listed on Business Periodicals Index.

Look for this massive service at the reference desk in your library. The information is updated monthly, a big help when you need to know what's new.

Also available is Wilson Business Abstracts which includes 150–250 word summaries for each article listed.

▶ **CompuServe:**   CompuServe, Inc.
5000 Arlington Centre Boulevard
P.O. Box 20212, Columbus, OH 43220
Telephone (800) 848-8199
Fax (614) 529-1610

CompuServe, a popular online information service that provides a wide range of less expensive database services, includes information retrieval on some databases that are likely to be useful in a job search.

Like other online services, CompuServe provides several news databases, such as Reuters, Associated Press, Business Wire, and *The Washington Post*. Full-text newspaper coverage includes 60 U.S. newspapers online; issues go back nearly ten years. For company data, CompuServe's available databases include Disclosure, InvesText, and Standard & Poor's.

CompuServe has a low monthly subscription fee and its per-minute online charge for certain databases is inexpensive.

▶ **Corporate Jobs Outlook!:**   Corporate Jobs Outlook, Inc.
P.O. Drawer 670466
Dallas, TX 75367
Telephone (214) 692-1085
Fax (214) 692-0105

Corporate Jobs Outlook! is a standout database. It is unique in that it analyzes everything job seekers want to know about each company: key executives, sales figures, earnings, salary and benefit ratings, financial stability rating, industry outlook, company, outlook, and opportunity estimates.

It contains the complete text of *Corporate Jobs Outlook!,* a newsletter about career opportunities at leading corporations. The product covers employers from 45 areas of business, including aerospace, banking, computers, insurance, pharmaceuticals, and retailing. It is updated every two months and is available online from NewsNet Inc. and The Human Resource Information Network.

▶ **CorpTech:**   Corporate Technology Information Services, Inc.
12 Alfred Street
Suite 200, Woburn, MA 01801
Telephone (800) 333-8036
Fax (617) 932-6335

Available in print, on diskette, on CD-ROM or online, the CorpTech Database can be used to identify employers of high-tech personnel. CorpTech profiles over 40,000 public and private U.S. manufacturers and developers of technology products.

▶ **Duns Million Dollar Disc:**   Dun & Bradstreet Information Services
One Diamond Hill Road
Murray Hill, NJ 07974
Telephone (800) 526-0651
Fax (201) 605-6911

Duns Million Dollar Disc, a CD-ROM product of Dun & Bradstreet Information Services, is a library reference costing several thousand dollars annually.

This service is a widely used resource for employer information. It contains information on more than 200,000 public and private U.S. companies.

It covers the economic spectrum of commercial, industrial, and business establishments, giving full details on geographical locations. The big plus for job seekers is that this Dun & Bradstreet product on corporate giants lists the names and business background of top management personnel.

You can search by industry, location, and a number of other criteria. Updated quarterly, this is a "gold standard" of corporate databases.

▶ **General BusinessFile, Public Edition:**   Information Access Company
362 Lakeside Drive
Foster City, CA 94404
Telephone (800) 227-8431
Fax (415) 378-5369

General BusinessFile is a CD-ROM product that bills itself as the only fully integrated database covering all aspects of business, management, company, and industry information.

It consolidates the most respected investment reports available and corporate profiles of public and (hard to find) private companies. It also includes wide-ranging, current business news from trade, industry, and management journals and newspapers.

Designed specifically to meet the needs of library users, General BusinessFile provides one-stop research on job hunting strategies, as well as other subjects such as investments, local and regional economic trends, consumer surveys, small business management, and new technologies and products.

Topics available for research are international trade, mergers and acquisitions, key industry and market trends, management theories, and general economics. The service is updated monthly.

▶ **Hoover's Handbooks:**   Reference Press, Inc.
6448 Highway 290E
Suite E-104, Austin, TX 78723
Telephone (512) 454-7778
Fax (512) 454-9401

This group of resources offers job seekers affordable information on more than 8,000 companies and 200 industries. The information comes in these formats:

Hoover's MasterList of America's Top 2,500 Employers is a book and disk combo that identifies the largest and the fastest-growing companies in the nation. Each entry shows company name, headquarters address, telephone and fax numbers, the names of the human resources executive and the chief executive officer, the number of employees, annual percentage change in employment and industry. The disk, bound into the back of the book, is a breeze to search and sort—by size, region, industry and so forth—to print letters and labels. At bookstores, it retails for less than $20.

Hoover's Electronic MasterList of Major U.S. Companies contains basic contact information on disk for more than 8,000 top U.S. companies for less than $200 (or less than $300 with quarterly updates). Not only more companies, but more data is presented on each company than the less expensive cousin above.

Hoover's Company and Industry Database on CD-ROM provides in-depth profiles of more than 1,500 of the largest and most rapidly growing companies both nationally and internationally, as well as profiles of more than 200 U.S. industries. It is ideal for locating potential employers and preparing for job interviews, offering the scoop on the companies' operations, officers, strategies, competitors, history, headquarters location, products and brand names, and up to 10 years of financial information. The cost to single users: about $250.

You can also find Hoover databases online: America Online (News and Finance area; keyword: "Hoover" or "Company"); CompuServe (keyword: "Go Hoover"); and other resources.

To receive an electronic catalog featuring dozens of reasonably priced references for job seekers, access the Internet's world wide web at this address: http://www.hoovers.com

▶ **Investext on InfoTrac:**   Information Access Company
                               362 Lakeside Drive
                               Foster City, CA 94404
                               Telephone (800) 227-8431
                               Fax (415) 378-5369

This service contains indexing or full text of some 30,000 company/industry reports. This covers over 11,000 U.S. and international companies in 53 industries. The data come from 270 of the world's leading investment banks, brokerage firms, and consulting and research firms.

Investext can be used to analyze a company's line(s) of business, check a company's financial health, and locate current and historical financial information.

▶ **Lexis/Nexis:**   P.O. Box 933
                     Dayton, OH 45401
                     Telephone (800) 227-4908
                     Fax (513) 865-6909

The Lexis/Nexis services are the world's premier full-text, online legal, news and business information services.

A pioneer in the online information industry, the Lexis service, the first commercial full-text legal information service, began in 1973 to help legal professionals research the law more efficiently. The Lexis service contains major archives of federal and state case law, continuously up-dated statues of all 50 states, state and federal regulations and public records from major U.S. states.

The Nexis service is the leading full-text news and business infor-mation service. It offers more than 5,800 sources of news and business in-formation and is unmatched in depth and breadth of information. Some 100,000 new articles are added daily from worldwide newspapers, maga-zines, news wires, and trade journals. The extensive array of news and in-formation options make this the service of choice for many journalists and researchers.

Pricing is flexible with hourly, transactional and subscription options available.

▶ **Martindale-Hubbell:**   Reed Reference Publishing Company
121 Chanlon Road
New Providence, NJ 07974
Telephone (800) 526-4902
Fax (908) 464-3553

Lawyers can cruise the Martindale-Hubbell Law Directory database to identify potential employers of legal counsel. Identified are more than 800,000 lawyers and law firms, in excess of 1,000 corporate law depart-ments, and 6,500 services and suppliers to the legal profession worldwide. This employer database, available in CD-ROM and online through the Lexis/Nexis, ideally illustrates services tailored for specific occupations. In this case, lawyers can search by state, county, city, name of firm, name of client, name of attorney, college, college year, law school, law school year, legal services, and much more.

The service, which is usually available at law libraries, university li-braries, and large public libraries, is updated quarterly on CD-ROM and throughout the year on Lexis/Nexis. (See Lexis/Nexis database service above.)

▶ **Moody's:**   99 Church Street
New York, NY 10007
Telephone (800) 342-5647
Fax (212) 553-4700

Moody's offers a number of electronic products of interest to job seekers. Among the CD-ROMS are *Moody's Company Data,* which identifies more than 10,000 U.S. based public companies; and *Moody's International Company Data,* which shows some 10,000 companies in about 90 other countries.

▶ **S&P CORPORATIONS:**   Standard & Poor's
25 Broadway
New York, NY 10004
Telephone (212) 208-8429
Fax (212) 412-0459

Another major service that may be available through a library's business reference desk is S&P CORPORATIONS. This comprehensive product contains descriptive details and financial data on U.S. and international corporations in three files:

1. *Executives* holds biographical profiles of more than 70,000 key personnel.
2. *Private Companies* profiles more than 45,000 leading private corporations.
3. *Public Companies* contains descriptive and financial data, including current financial news on 12,000 publicly traded companies.

This service is available as a CD-ROM disc through Standard & Poor's, a division of the McGraw-Hill Companies, or through KR Information OnDisc, part of Knight-Ridder Information, Inc.

▶ **The Business Elite:**   Database America
100 Paragon Drive
Montvale, NJ 07645
Telephone (800) 223-7777
Fax (201) 476-2405

This database provides in-depth information on 500,000 of America's largest corporations in today's business-to-business marketplace. It offers the following fields of data: company name, address, telephone, stock exchange by type, fortune company indicator, 8-digit SIC and business description, sales volume, employment size, executive name and title, and more.

The Business Elite features unlimited downloading. It is available on CD-ROM.

▶ **The Job Finder's Tool Kit:**   Planning/Communications
7215 Oak Avenue
River Forest, IL 60305
Telephone (800) 829-5220
Fax: (708) 366-5280

This extensive, pleasant-to-use program is a compilation of three popular guidebooks in the Job Finder series: *Professional's Private Sector Job Finder, Non-Profits' Job Finder,* and *Government Job Finder.* All are published by Planning/Communications in the spring of even-numbered years.

It is available on 3.5" floppies, or as a CD-ROM, and reports on more than 5,500 sources that can lead you to hundreds of thousands of job vacancies. Sources include many job hotlines, job-matching services, online job or resume databases, job bulletin boards, specialty and trade periodicals, and directories. The CD-ROM version includes a 45-minute video where the author gives insightful advice on conducting an effective job search.

The floppy disk version requires more than 12 megabytes of space on your hard drive.

Career fields available in the Tool Kit cover the waterfront, ranging from education, environment, health care, social services, and teaching, to engineering, nonprofit foundation management, higher education, legal services, music and dance, and school administration.

The product also includes descriptions of salary surveys and job search advice on writing cover letters and resumes, and on interviewing.

There are two ways to use The Job Finder's Tool Kit. One is to simply browse through it by clicking on the forward arrow. The most effective way is to select "search" and type in the occupation for which you want to find job vacancies. You'll get a list of every place in Lauber's three books where the target term appears. You can easily zip right over to each job source. You then can print out the results of your search simply by clicking the printer icon. You can easily copy the results of your search to your word processor or your database.

The Job Finder's Tool Kit sparkles on government search assignments, listing what is probably the most complete compendium of resources for government jobs at local, state, and federal levels.

▶ **Companies International:**   Gale Research, Inc.,
835 Penobscot Building
Detroit, MI 48226
Telephone (800) 347-4253
Fax (313) 961-6815

Companies International is another CD-ROM you should look for at a library reference desk. This annual service profiles more than 140,000 public and private U.S. companies including difficult-to-track, privately-held firms, and also includes information on more than 200,000 international companies. Top executives are listed, as well as the number of employees, revenue, and industry.

This CD-ROM corresponds to the five-volume printed *Ward's Business Directory of U.S. Private & Public Companies* and to the *World Trade Centers Association World Business Directory.*

ELECTRONIC RESEARCH SERVICE BUREAUS

Perhaps now you appreciate the big boost an electronic search can give your career. But let's face it: Not all of us are crazy about using computers for anything. As one wag says, "If builders built buildings the way programmers write programs, then the first woodpecker that came along would destroy civilization."

If you dread the thought of firing up a computer and becoming an instant expert on information search, why not hire an electronic researcher to do the computer legwork for you?

Electronic researchers are combination computer and research whizzes who can produce highly accurate job lead lists.

Because job search electronic research is a fairly new occupation, you may need to call around and check backgrounds to find the best researcher for you.

You may be able to locate job search electronic researchers—also called job market information consultants—by asking at your library or college career center.

Hiring a job search electronic researcher will cost you between about $65 to $150 an hour. Some charge a minimum fee of $500 or more. Often, you won't have to spend more than $100 to $200 for a customized list of target companies and recruiters.

It may sound expensive but there is a learning curve for each database, and the wrong keystroke with an online system can be costly because most online services charge by the minute.

If you need more justification in your desire to avoid computers, one information consultant points out, "Your goal is to land a job, not learn how to research."

Before you put money on the electronic researcher's table, observe these common sense rules:

1. Check references of former clients. Call and ask whether the data supplied by the electronic researcher were relatively valid and current—or whether they were filled with information so out-of-date it was easily confused with bleu cheese.

2. Check whether any complaints were filed with the Better Business Bureau or the state consumer protection office.

3. Ask the researchers for specifics on the data you're buying. What databases are used? How large are they? How often are they updated? Unless you're in an obscure occupation, a benchmark is that your search should be conducted in databases of more than 200,000 companies.

4. Get a clear understanding *in writing* of what it will cost you.

5. Be clear in your mind about one thing: You are not buying a list of companies with job openings. The electronic researchers have no way of knowing who is hiring and who is not. They are providing you with a list of *prospective* employers or recruiters who may or may not be able to advance your job search. That's all. For this reason, it's difficult to establish a meaningful refund policy.

6. Find out how you will receive the data—paper, fax, diskette, modem. Once a researcher has the raw material to shape your search, the data can be organized in many ways—by geographic location, industry ranking, sales, number of employees, years in business, and so forth.

   Some electronic research service bureaus, for an additional charge, will create mailing packages of letters (from letters you compose), envelopes, or labels.

Suppose you don't get more than ten really good leads. Should you get a refund because you didn't get twenty really good leads? Or hundreds of really good leads? You'll have to think about this and decide what information you must receive to make your investment worthwhile.

As an example, here is a firm that will handle your action in finding the employers or recruiters who deal in your type of job.

▶ **Pro/File Research:**   P.O. Box 602
                         Flourtown, PA 19031
                         Telephone (215) 643-3411
                         Fax (215) 643-3626

This electronic research service bureau is a prime example of the new breed of specialists who encourage you to "Leave the searching to us." The firm can identify companies venture and capital firms and executive recruiting firms of interest—as specified by you. In addition to individuals, career counselors often call Pro/File Research to prepare job lead packages for their clients.

A new and interesting feature is a service to assist the "trailing" spouse of a transferred employee.

When a spouse is transferred by a company, the employer usually offers assistance with real estate, moving expenses, and travel, but some firms add a program of spousal job placement assistance.

Pro/File Research can access a database of some 10 million employers and 4,500 + executive recruiters and 1,300 venture capital firms to identify all the possible employers in the requested parameters within a designated geographic area.

In a recent search, a spouse wanted a list of manufacturers of fabricated metal products with at least 200 employees, located in an area of eastern Massachusetts and northern Rhode Island that was within commuting distance from the spouse's new home.

The Pro/File Research package turned up 91 companies. We don't know whether a job jackpot was the result—most electronic researchers never hear the end of the story unless they make a special effort to follow up. Most of the 91 companies won't pan out, but several could be perfect job leads. Can you imagine the time saved by electronic search? Impressive!

As another plus for job seekers, Pro/File Research offers a laser-printed envelope service that matches the addresses on the list of recruiters and target companies, as well as cover letters that use the job seeker's text.

You advise this service what sort of employer you're looking for and where you'd like to locate, and you provide the text for the communications. Next, all you do is stuff the printed envelopes that the service has addressed with your tailor-made letters to the companies you selected, lick the stamps, and drop the stamped envelopes into the mail. Then pray that if you don't strike oil with an immediate opening, the companies use applicant tracking systems that will cherish and save your resumes.

Pro/File also assists people starting businesses locate business customers.

INFORMATION BROKERS WITH JOB SEARCH EXPERIENCE

In addition to an electronic research service bureau whose employees do nothing but job search, here are selected information brokers across the nation who have experience preparing job lead lists and doing literature search (researching information from articles, annual reports, and other sources for interviews).

Although this is not a complete list, we have compiled it with the aid of reliable information professionals. Prices depend on many factors, so confirm costs in advance of a search with each information broker.

Susanne Bjorner
Bjorner & Associates
7 Tamarack Lane
Woodbury, CT 06798
Telephone (203) 263-4759
Fax (203) 263-0278

Burwell Enterprises
Helen Burwell
3724 F.M. 1960 West No. 214
Houston, TX 77068
Telephone (713) 537-9051
Fax (713) 537-8332

Cooper Hydock Rugge (East)
Linda Cooper
622 South 42nd Street
Philadelphia, PA 19104
Telephone (215) 823-5490
Fax (215) 823-5493

Cooper Hydock Rugge (West)
Jim Hydock
3286 Adeline Street
Berkeley, CA 94703
Telephone (510) 420-0800
Fax (510) 420-0804

Corporate Fact Finders
Sharon Dean
884 Westtown Road
West Chester, PA 19382
Telephones (800) 220-3228; (610) 431-3708
Fax (610) 431-0674

MarketingBase
Amelia Kassel
1364 Kathy Lane
Sebastopol, CA 95472
Telephones (800) 544-5924; (707) 829-9421
Fax (707) 823-2713

Martin Goffman Associates
Dr. Martin Goffman
3 Dellview Drive
Edison, NJ 08820
Telephone (908) 549-5433
Fax (908) 906-1687

Notes Unlimited
Cliff Williams
14301 Swan Lane
Gulfport, MS 39503
Telephones (800) 729-4491; (601) 832-8731
Fax (601) 831-3045

The Information Consultancy
Mary Park
308 Tunbridge Road
Baltimore, MD 21212
Telephone (410) 532-7275
Fax (410) 433-8793

YOUR VISION OF THE FUTURE

Wonderous, isn't it—how the new electronic employer databases can produce customized products for you, to your specifications?

These opportunities come just in the nick of time for the ambitious manager and professional competing in a new information-technology-driven global marketplace.

Take your cue from a favorite old French saying that admonishes would-be travelers to chart their course before setting out:

What! No star, and you are going out to sea?
Marching, and you have no music?
Traveling, and you have no map?

Speaking collectively of the electronic databases just described: THIS is your map!

6 The Computerized Job Interview

When Computers Greet You at the Door, Take Your Application, and Test Your Skills

In previous chapters, we focused on the matchmaking aspects of job search—how people and jobs find each other. In this chapter, we focus on what happens after they find each other.

Interviewing often is done in two basic stages: screening and selection. Human resource specialists typically do the screening, making sure that applicants are qualified for the position in question. Managers to whom the new employee would report usually do the selection interviews.

This chapter will make you aware of how the functions involved in the screening interview—which may or may not include filling out application forms and having your skills and integrity tested—are circling around computers.

Two basic models exist. The first begins with human contact, moving to a computer interview; the second begins with a computer application, moving to human contact. Skill and integrity testing can be a part of either model.

A new type of software with artificial intelligence permits you to drill in job interview techniques until effective responses are second nature.

Imagine this: You see a help-wanted ad, respond, are invited to fill out an application form and then are asked to return the next morning for a job interview. So far, so good—a routine approach.

When you return the following morning, the receptionist says, "Follow me," and you do, expecting to be greeted by a smiling interviewer. Your mouth is open to say "Nice office" when you notice that the receptionist has escorted you to an empty room. There's nothing, and no one, in it—except for a computer terminal sitting on a stand. The computer isn't smiling, and it couldn't care less about your impression of the decor.

Why are you and the terminal being left alone in the room? The receptionist explains. Your initial screening interview, the first cut that separates the good bets from the near misses, will be conducted by a computer! A bit different—not so routine an approach.

Has hiring come to this? Are people going to be judged by machines? No, but for certain jobs in some corporations, computers are supplementing the human resource staff by giving human interviewers a hand. Computers help, but, thank heavens, people still hire people.

Here's what happens during a typical computer-assisted interview.

You sit at a terminal and work through a series of some 50 to 100 multiple-choice questions about employment history, job qualifications, and general background.

Once you're finished, you'll be asked to wait a few minutes before you have the opportunity to speak with a human interviewer. What you may not realize is that the job application you filled out yesterday was fed into a computer. It is compared to a printout of data obtained from the computerized interview you just completed. Do the answers look as though they came from the same person? Are there glaring differences? An evaluation is made.

A human interviewer checks the evaluation. It shows not only the answers you gave, but which questions took you an unusually long time to answer. The evaluation red-flags areas of concern the human interviewer should probe. To the question "Is it okay to take damaged goods?," for example, the interviewer will no doubt want to pursue a response of "It depends."

As we noted, the computerized interview includes questions you previously answered on the application form; it may ask the same questions in different ways to see whether your answers match.

Suppose on your application you say you are a high school graduate, but in the computer interview you add that you have "some college." The interviewer will want to know why you gave different answers. Or, in the interview, one question asks about standing on your feet for prolonged time spans and you say it will aggravate a back problem, but in answering another question, you say it will not be a problem to lift 30-pound boxes. The interviewer will certainly want to probe this disparity.

HOW HAS COMPUTER-ASSISTED INTERVIEWING HELD UP?

Since 1978, when the first person to be interviewed by a computer for a job made history at Corbin Ltd., a sewing factory in Huntington, West Virginia, more than 6 million job applicants have followed in her keystrokes.

The Greentree Computer-Assisted Employment Interview was the first of its kind and has evolved over a 17-year history to its present prominence.

The majority of users of this system—now operated by its developer, Brooks Mitchell, PhD, president of Aspen Tree Software, Inc. in Laramie, Wyoming—are hotels and retailers, hospitals, teleprocessing operators, and many other employers who hire large volumes of people.

We find this to be a relatively fair interviewing method because everyone is asked the same questions in the same way, and most of the questions dig beneath the surface for attitudes and personal traits. You can win by being consistent and by not hesitating over questions of honesty and ethics.

Most corporate users of computer-assisted employment interviews report improvements in the personnel selection process in such areas as worker turnover, absenteeism, theft, and productivity. A consensus among users reportedly points to an overall improvement in the quality of the employee hired because the computer helps decision makers overcome problems inherent in the traditional job interview. These problems include judgment factors among interviewers and the consistency of their questions.

What are we talking about here, a kind of pilot error syndrome among interviewers? Possibly. Research indicates disadvantages of the human-to-human interview do exist. Interviewers' errors include: forgetting to ask important questions, talking too much, being reluctant to ask sensitive questions, forming unjustified negative first impressions, obtaining unreliable information that makes an applicant feel unfairly judged, and using interview data ineffectively.

By contrast, a computer-assisted employment interview, say its proponents, creates a good interview because it incorporates many of the skills and experiences of seasoned interviewers and avoids the recognizable pitfalls of human-to-human interviews.

Advocates of computer interviewing say computers present job applicants with questions that, although they are multiple-choice, do require reflection. The computer is programmed to spot inconsistent or problematic answers.

Here's a sampling of computer interview questions:

1. George, if you were given a supervisory position, how would you evaluate your chances for success?

    A. Very poor; this would not be a good job for me.

    B. Poor; I don't think I would perform well.

    C. Fair; I think I could do an adequate job.

    D. Good; I think I would perform above average.

    E. Excellent; I think I would be highly successful.

    F. I am not sure how I would perform.

2. George, how would you rate your performance at the Acme Brick Company?

    A. Very poor.

    B. Poor.

    C. Fair.

    D. Good.

    E. Excellent.

    F. I'm not sure.

3. George, could we have your permission to contact Sam Katz [George's previous supervisor] to see how he would rate your job performance at the Acme Brick Company?

    A. Yes.

    B. Possibly.

    C. No.

Greentree experts explain that people would rather talk to a computer than a person, especially in sensitive subject areas. Let that piece of information be a clue: Don't tell a computer anything you would not reveal to a human interviewer. The computer won't keep your secrets.

Why do people respond more honestly to a computer than to a human interviewer? Partly because the computer is a peerless interviewer—ageless and sexless—and thus less suspect and threatening than a human interviewer. Job hunters may not feel embarrassed to respond to a computer because they know it won't be shocked or disappointed by their response. One university study reveals that when applicants admit to a computer the amount of alcohol they put away, it is higher than the amount they describe to a human interviewer.

The following information frequently is contained in the computer-generated report human interviewers receive before the face-to-face meeting:

- *Response summary.* This item summarizes the job applicant's responses and categorizes them under such major headings as work history and life experience.

- *Contradictory responses.* The applicant may have indicated he or she was terminated from the most recent job because of poor attendance; at a later point in the interview, he or she may indicate that an outstanding recommendation was received from a former employer.

- *Late responses.* When an applicant takes longer than average (as measured by the applicant's own average time of response) to answer, responses to those questions are itemized.

- *Potential problems.* This category identifies problem answers in areas predetermined by the employer. A response indicating the applicant intends to remain on the job for less than a year would be clearly highlighted for the interviewer as a problem response.

- *Suggested questions for interviewer.* These questions, which are preconstructed by the employer, are chosen for each applicant based on his or her responses to the multiple-choice questions. For example, the computer may prompt the interviewer to ask, "George, you mentioned that you feel a previous employer would rate your performance as average. Why don't you feel it would be higher?" This feature ensures additional control and consistency of the job interview.

A number of Fortune 1000 companies are adding the computer-assisted interviewing process to their human resource departments: Marriott Hotels, NordicTrack, American Express, Neiman Marcus, American General Insurance, The Perrier Group of America, Corning Glass, and Kaiser Permanente are among those using this innovative technique.

What about the next generation of computer-assisted interviewing? According to Dr. Brooks Mitchell: "Without question, it's *interactive video* to draw insights as to how a person would react to certain situations." Dr. Mitchell's research demonstrates that applicants give different responses when they see something, as opposed to when they read something. "Videos convey far more nuances and subtleties then the written word," he explains.

To learn more about The Greentree Computer-Assisted Employment Interview, contact Aspen Tree Software, Inc., P.O. Box 1347, Laramie, WY 82070; Telephone (307) 721-5888; Fax (307) 721-2135.

Dovetail is another well regarded and comprehensive computerized interviewing program that major companies are using to screen job applicants. This software package is a product of and marketed by The Dovetail Group in Atlanta.

The Dovetail Computer Interview program is multi-faceted and many-splendored; it is designed to assist the face-to-face human interviewer with a highly focused and structured interview. Dovetail contains assessment and profiling features.

(Human resource readers will want to know that, like some of the programs described in Chapter 3, Dovetail is a full-service HR resource, offering an applicant tracking capability, a database search feature, automatic letter-writing power, plus other useful personnel office tools. Dovetail departs from other computerized interview programs in that it allows the human resource specialist to compare every applicant to a company-specific database of employees in various profiles—low turnover, high performance, and so on. This feature further guides the face-to-face interviewer through detailed and intense discussions.)

From the job applicant's standpoint, the use of Dovetail's computerized programs suggest greater scrutiny is being given to your quest for the position. All the "t's" are being crossed and all the "i's" dotted.

From the human resource specialist's standpoint, Dovetail is designed to give a kind of infrared scope to use in the dark areas of choosing the best person for the job.

Dovetail Software can be reached at 11 Piedmont Center, Suite 810, Atlanta, GA 30305; Telephone (800) 421-2341; Fax (404) 262-9167.

WHEN APPLYING FOR A JOB IS LIKE GETTING CASH AT AN ATM

Remember when you had to wait in line to see a teller to get cash out of your bank? And remember how you learned to save time when withdrawing cash by learning to follow the menus on an automatic teller machine (ATM)?

Well, now you can do something like that in applying for a job. As an example, a large bank that hires 50 new people on the average each week, has installed the Restrac Kiosk system to provide "job applications on demand." It's like an ATM for job applications.

The kiosks are used to accept applications from walk-in applicants. Job seekers sit in front of a computer and fill out their applications.

Suppose you are the applicant. You are asked a question and given space to keyboard the answer. Succeeding questions are based on your answers to previous questions, just like an ATM asks you different questions after you tell it whether you are there to make a deposit or a withdrawal. Finished? You're asked to review your application and okay it. When you do, your application is whisked away into the bank's applicant tracking system.

It may take a little getting used to. For those of you who appreciate teller machines, you'll love it right off the bat. Especially if your handwriting is not easily read.

The bank's Restrac Kiosk system, produced by the same company that makes applicant tracking systems, may prove to be a harbinger of the future for large organizations and corporations that are inundated with thousands of job seekers each year.

For human resource specialists, it is a tremendous savings of time and human effort, as well as paper, which adds up to a lot of energy and natural resources.

For more information on The Restrac Kiosk System, contact Restrac Enterprise, 1 Dedham Place, Dedham, MA 02026; Telephone (617) 320-5600; Fax (617) 320-5630.

COMPUTERIZE YOUR HEAD FOR BETTER INTERVIEWS

Do you dread interviews? Here's help! In addition to practicing before a video camera to iron out the wrinkles of defeating personal mannerisms (fiddling with your hair, swinging your legs), you can upgrade your job interviewing performance by letting a computer coach you with verbal responses.

Interview Xpress, a computerized self-tutor that helps you become a whiz at job interviewing, isn't perfect. But it's a dramatically good way to bring managers and professional job seekers to grips with the intensity of preparation needed in today's highly competitive job market where 100 equally qualified applicants compete for one position.

Interview Xpress is modestly-priced software that organizes your mind through endless questioning. The questioning is not rote—something you could get from a book. Instead, the software uses artificial intelligence (AI) to challenge your answers until they're more likely to impress employers. The AI software is based on the knowledge of interviewing experts and is programmed to continue in different creative ways prompted by your individual response.

If, for instance, the Interviewer Xpress program asks why you want to work for a particular company and your answer lacks substance in a specific area, the software suggests you return to the question and sharpen your answer. Suppose you said you want to work for a particular company because it is near your home. The software requests that you add to your answer. You then respond with something about the company's fine reputation, or solid earnings records. You aren't let off the hook until you produce an acceptable answer to a given question.

After you've practiced your answers in one session, you can print them. The printout from a second self-tutoring session will not be identical, because your responses are apt to vary and carry you along different "branches of the inquiry road."

For details, contact Xpress P.S.S., Suite 100, 10001 Meadowbrook Drive, Dallas, Texas 75229; Telephone (214) 373-4742.

HONESTLY, CAN YOU BE TRUSTED?

If you're going after a job in which you handle money or are in a position to pilfer goods, you may meet up with a computerized Pinkerton interview.

A number of large to midsize corporations employ one of the leading security firms, Pinkerton Security and Investigation Services, to screen and process job applicants, particularly when integrity is paramount.

Pinkerton offers to corporate America computerized interviewing and screening services that are designed to keep a company from taking on a bad hire, especially one who will pocket money or goods.

Beyond the honesty factor, a number of Pinkerton's clients say they use these evaluations because they result in significant reductions in turnover and workers' compensation.

At the heart of its extensive applicant screening process is Pinkerton's IntelliView program. IntelliView is a telephone-administered, computerized, structured interview you do using a Touch-Tone phone. The interview is in three parts:

1. A preliminary interview conducted with a computer. About 100 questions are asked in less than 10 minutes. The questions probe your past work history and attitudes that may affect your productivity.

2. An "interview folder" provides the interviewer with an organized method of documenting the telephone interview answers. It contains space to note your biographical information, work history, and reference evaluation. It also lists specific follow-up questions—based on answers you gave during the computer interview—to ask during the face-to-face interview.

3. A follow-up, face-to-face interview that focuses on your "key interview responses" to the computer interview.

Pinkerton says more than 1 million applicants each year use some form of pre-employment evaluation.

Company officials report more than 60 percent of applicants successfully pass through Pinkerton's extensive and intensive interview process.

Want more information? Contact Pinkerton's Information Center, 6100 Fairview Road, Suite 900, Charlotte, NC 28210; Telephone (800) 232-PINK; Fax (704) 554-1806.

EMPLOYMENT TESTS YOU MAY FACE

Because testing—as a part of screening—can knock you out of the box no matter how well you do in all other areas of the job search, you should know a few things about the tests you may be asked to take.

These aren't substance abuse tests. We're talking about the kind of quizzing you're likely to encounter when you interact with a computer.

Most thoughtful people agree that tests can never be free from bias. In a classic example, a whole class of Hawaiian kids flunked an intelligence test because, when asked to draw a house, not one drew a chimney. The explanation is simple: In their climate, none had ever seen a chimney.

Employment testing is with us to stay, and here are a few of the most prevalent types.

Integrity Tests

Employers want to find out whether you're light-fingered. Employee pilferage—not to mention embezzlement—costs businesses billions of dollars yearly.

Balanced against that understandable concern regarding your tendencies toward honesty are your right to privacy and the validity of the testing.

The integrity exams usually are not tricky. They go right to the point, asking frankly about theft or deception. What's amazing is how people will incriminate themselves on "impersonal" tests, as though it's okay to tell a computer anything.

Experts say high-risk persons rate themselves lower in honesty and in such related areas as use of illegal drugs than do others. The thieves among us tend to believe that most employees steal and make easy excuses for theft. ("Everybody does it.") They often think about stealing and make more admissions of petty theft than do others.

Some people who overrate their ability to outfox the test will, by being too goody-goody in their answers, reveal to test interpreters that they are purposely trying to affect the test results.

Here are some examples of true/false questions designed to unmask attempts at distorting results:

- I don't worry what others think of me.
- I've never stolen anything in my life.
- I've never stolen from an employer.
- I've never cheated on a test.
- I've never even considered cheating.
- I never have trouble sleeping at night.

If you try answering "true" to all of the above statements, you signal that you're faking it. Haven't you ever swiped a donut or a pencil? Haven't you at least considered cribbing on a test? Haven't you ever had a restless night?

Test publishers say no single answer is used as a basis of conclusions; instead, they look for a tendency shown in a series of answers throughout the test. Be aware of your tendencies in the types of responses you give.

Test critics say that the honesty tests are genuinely predictive only when big numbers of people are involved, and that user companies play the percentages. This means, to paraphrase scholars on the issue, that innocent people will be misclassified and wrongly denied jobs.

How can you protect yourself?

When you are asked to take an integrity test, ask how the results will be used. This inquiry opens the door for your follow-up statement:

"I'm sure you know there is some disagreement about the value of integrity tests, and that false positives sometimes occur. I think I read that somewhere. I'm very interested in this job. Will you let me know if anything negative should turn up on my test, so I can have the opportunity to speak to that concern? I don't expect anything, but I like to cover all the bases when there's something I really want. That's fair, isn't it?"

Job Skills Tests

"Can you do the job?" is the question behind job skills testing. The test may require hands-on performance or may involve a computerized exam.

Try to determine what most employers use as a job skills test, and anticipate how you can brush up for it. You can't study for the tests an employer will give; they're not like examinations of knowledge. But by being aware of what may be asked, you probably can better handle the pressure of being tested.

Personality Tests

You're good, but are you normal? That's what employers want to know when they require you to take a psychological test as part of your screening process.

Questions on personality tests are designed to pin down vocational interest traits—and to make sure you won't disturb the peace in the work environment even if you can do the job.

After you complete the personality test, the company ends up with a psychological profile of you which, accurate or not, can be used in decisions to hire, promote, or eventually fire you.

Computers are used to measure your raw scores against a "normative" group—people who have taken the test previously. If a group of successful engineers, for instance, tended to answer the test questions in a certain way, and you, as an engineer, answer those questions in the same way, you will be presumed to have the personality of a successful engineer.

The predictive validity of these tests depends on those for whom the tests were standardized. With our culture undergoing rapid change— by the year 2000, nearly 30 percent of the U.S. population will be members of minorities—it's a challenge for test makers to stay current.

"There is a great deal of old-fashionedness built into these tests . . . cultural lag," according to William H. Whyte, author of *The Organization Man,* one of the blockbuster management books of the 1950s.

"They don't dare change the doggone things because then they can't say, 'We have tested this against 50,000 supervisory personnel.' The minute they change one question, they no longer can make that claim."

Whyte has interpreted this to mean that "unconsciously, the framers of the tests have enshrined the attitudes of some years ago."

Some people subscribe to the be-yourself school of testing. They say it's unwise to attempt to beat the personality tests by telling employers what you think they want to hear.

We're not so sure. An equally valid approach is to write a clear, concise personality statement in advance of job hunting. Declare who you think you are. Include your characteristics. List your strengths as they apply to the job you hope to land. Write as though you were describing a character in a film script.

Other job applicants are more cynical. They approach personality tests by forming a clear mental picture of a very successful friend in a similar career field. Then they concentrate on what they think their friend's attitudes would be toward the questions. This technique works for some people.

When it's personality test time, try to make your answers consistent for the character you have described, or to the mental image of a successful friend. It's wise to stay in character—but tilt toward conservatism.

If, for instance, you see such questions as "Which do you read first, (a) the financial pages or (b) the sports section?," or "Would you prefer to spend an afternoon (a) chopping wood or (b) digging ditches?" try to answer in a manner best fitting your character.

Here's one more tip to ace psychological tests: Avoid absolutes in answering most questions. The words "always" or "never" can be a trap. For example, "I've never taken more than my fair share of anything" should be marked false or you may be seen as too good to be true.

7

Bedknobs, Broomsticks, and Job-Seeking Wizardry

A Collage of High-Tech Tools for Choosing a Career, Landing a Job, and Moving Up

In this chapter, we review a medley of electronic services for today's job market, developments that are excitingly new to most of us. The chapter ends with a preview of emerging technologies that will take our job searches further than ever before.

Think about the electronic revolution this way: Do you prefer that technology befriend or bedevil you?

Radical change is sweeping the job market—beyond even the dramatic developments we've explored in the preceding chapters.

Here are more changes. Some are measured in baby steps. Others have blockbuster potential. Even if you are not actively seeking a new job as you read, take this chance to get the high-tech lowdown on new ways to make the job market work for you. In a few words, make technology your new best friend. Finally, anticipate, with us, the beckoning job search frontier so that you can take good care of your future.

PASS THE TELEPHONE

We don't have to remind you that the telephone is one of the principal and most important tools in your job search. However, you may want information about some new and inexpensive resources via Uncle Alexander's little invention—resources that can make your life more interesting and possibly a lot easier as you embark on the hunt for your next job.

Career America Connection

How it benefits you: For the cost of a telephone call, usually less than $2 or $3 in long-distance charges, you can find out about all the open federal jobs for which you qualify. This is a real red-tape cutter and an admirable example of your tax dollars at work.

Many people still don't know about this first-rate federal government service. Career America Connection is a telephone system (you pay for long-distance calls) but it can be a real time saver, and time is money. The average call is about six minutes in length, at a typical cost of 25 cents or less per minute.

The U.S. Office of Personnel Management developed this system. Anyone interested in available federal jobs can call any day of the week, 24 hours a day, on either a rotary or Touch-Tone telephone. Make sure you have a pad of paper and a pencil or pen handy because lots of information is packed into a short amount of time.

After you're connected, you'll be asked to choose from a menu of options. Touch-Tone telephone users punch buttons on the dialing pad; rotary callers use voice commands the system will recognize. This means you just touch or talk your way to the information you want.

Career America Connection has two job information services: Career America College Hotline and the General Jobline.

The College Hotline contains information on entry-level jobs for college graduates nationwide. (This same information is available free at college career centers, job fairs, and public job service offices.)

College Hotline callers choose from such occupational categories as accounting, administrative, business and finance, engineering, law enforcement, medical and health careers, and science.

Although this service is aimed primarily at recent graduates, more seasoned job seekers who are considering entry-level or junior-level government positions can benefit by using the College Hotline.

The General Jobline adds to the College Hotline information, discussing jobs across the country at all levels.

"Job openings" are announcements of actual positions to be filled, but often the government lists "job opportunities" for anticipated openings within the near future at specific agencies. These opportunities announcements are usually a good indication that job openings will soon exist.

An example of this outcome occurred in 1981, when President Reagan threatened to fire striking FAA air traffic controllers. The "opportunities" announcement heralding the possibility of openings in the air traffic control field went out. A few days later, Reagan did what he promised and the "job opportunities" announcement was switched to a "job openings" announcement. The "job openings" announcement was posted for job vacancies that actually existed. The anticipation had become reality.

"Job opportunities" should be studied and considered as a good indication of what's in the wings. It's your cue to prepare and apply.

In addition to job openings and opportunities, callers can choose messages about federal salaries and benefits, how federal jobs are filled, special employment programs for veterans and people with disabilities, and student and intern programs. The information is fresh because it's updated daily.

Another plus for Career America Connection is that you're invited to leave voice-mail messages with your contact information, to receive application materials. These messages are processed the next business day so you'll probably get the information within a week.

Call Career America Connection at (912) 757-3000.

Career America Connection covers the range of jobs available throughout the federal government at any given time. Some departments and agencies of the government operate their own hotlines to maintain a tighter rein on their individual recruiting efforts. An example of a single agency hotline is the one operated by the Library of Congress in Washington.

The telephone number for the Library of Congress electronic job line is (202) 707-4315.

A DATABASE DESCRIBING FEDERAL JOBS

Considering the thousands of jobs and classifications within the federal government, you definitely need a road map to find where you're trying to go. What kinds of jobs are there today? In what department or agency?

What are the requirements? The pay? The geographic location? Must you take a test?

For answers to questions like these, here is a program to help you cut through the bureaucratic maze of the federal government.

FOCIS

How it benefits you: Here's an easy way to get the scoop on federal job descriptions.

The Federal Occupational and Career Information System (FOCIS), a database, gives you a better handle on various occupations within the federal government.

You can look through library reference books, or you can go to most public employment service offices, college career centers, or your library, and ask to use the computer-driven FOCIS, Version 4. Or you can purchase the diskette yourself.

Prepared by the Office of Personnel Management, FOCIS describes more than 360 federal white-collar occupations likely to have the largest number of openings. Remember, these aren't actual openings; they are job descriptions in agencies where openings are likely to be frequent.

For each occupation, FOCIS gives a description of the work, minimum qualifications, grade levels, salaries, and addresses to contact.

Campus career center staffs across the nation are using electronics to put graduates together with employers. This program comes on a disk for use on personal computers. For a recorded message with details, call the National Technical Information Service at (703) 487-4650.

Job Hotlines USA

How would you like to have more than 2,000 hard-to-find telephone numbers offering prerecorded lists of available jobs at companies and government agencies? For less that $30, including shipping, you can buy a copy of *Job Hotlines USA, The National Telephone Directory of Employer Joblines* from Career Communications Inc., 298 Main Street, P.O. Box 169, Harleysville, PA 19438; Telephone (800) 346-1848. Your library may have a copy.

Most joblines are not toll-free 800 numbers, but they are typically available 24 hours a day and you can save money by calling during off-peak hours and weekends. Have paper and pencil ready when you call.

CRAMMING FOR MORE THAN JUST FINAL EXAMS

If you're a recent college graduate, you don't have to be told that it's tough sledding on a crowded hill for that first job—particularly if you were a liberal arts major. Here's what a couple of leading universities are doing to help their graduates get jobs.

JobWeb

This Internet World Wide Web site (http://www.jobweb.org) is a stunning and comprehensive resource for college students and experienced alumni who are in the midst of a job search, for employers who hire college graduates, and for campus career services practitioners who guide students in their employment quests.

As competition for the best jobs becomes razor sharp, savvy graduates will find this indispensable resource arriving just in time.

JobWeb, a service of the not-for-profit National Association of Colleges and Employers (formerly the College Placement Council) in Bethlehem, Pennsylvania, includes job openings and employer descriptions, a resume database, and several newsgroups (online interactive discussion groups). It is a virtual office where a variety of professional issues and concerns are discussed. Among the multitude of future services JobWeb will offer are videoconferencing, multimedia shows, and interactive training opportunities.

JobWeb is developing so rapidly that your best bet is to check at your college's career services office for ways to use it in your job search.

By any measure, JobWeb is in the top tier of electronic services changing the face of job search in America.

Southeastern Atlantic Coast Career Network

How it benefits you: For graduating college seniors, here's new interactive videoconferencing technology that permits interviews across town or across the country. This may mean more employers will be interested in you because they don't have to send a representative to your campus or fly you to headquarters for an interview unless they're fairly sure you're a strong candidate for hire. The technology may ultimately enhance employment chances for graduates of smaller colleges to which employers do not normally send recruiters.

SEACnet stands for Southeastern Atlantic Coast Career Network. At press time, it is the working title of a consortium of 22 public and private university career centers.

They are:

University of Alabama

Auburn University

Clemson University

Duke University

Florida State University

University of Florida

Georgia Institute of Technology

University of Georgia

University of Kentucky

Louisiana State University

University of Georgia

University of Kentucky

Louisiana State University

University of Maryland

Mississippi State University

North Carolina State University

University of North Carolina

University of South Carolina

University of Tennessee

Vanderbilt University

University of Virginia

Wake Forest University

The consortium's videoconferencing technology connects employers with students in ways never before possible, says Dr. Drema Howard of the University of Kentucky. Here's how the system works:

1. Employers can search for student candidates by major/degree, or by state, or by university.

2. Employers can leave a job vacancy posting on SEACnet for students to see. (Some of the job openings also will appear on the national database of *JobWeb,* the service of the National Association of Colleges and Employers. Other job vacancies in this database will be listed only in target colleges and universities in the Southeastern Atlantic area. And not every consortium participant will have every job listing. Remember, employers call the shots when deciding where to list jobs. It's too early in the unrolling of this electronic option to know with certainty whether recruiting ranges will expand now that the cost-effective videoconferencing technology is available.)

3. Employers can forward a job vacancy listing to consortium member university career services offices asking for resumes that meet the job's hiring criteria.

4. Employers can schedule a videoconferencing interview at a university.

5. Employers and students can see and hear each other as well as view a resume online and highlight items of importance. Either party can transmit or receive data. Either party can simultaneously utilize a mouse or keyboard.

As a graduating senior at one of the consortium's members, you can go to your university's career services office and enter your resume in the electronic database. (The particulars depend upon which electronic system your university is using; this information is readily available at your career services office.)

You can also search the system for job openings you like and follow up on them. Here's a scenario of how the SEACnet system is expected to function.

Accessing the SEACnet (Internet World Wide Web) website, a hypothetical company we'll call Edjali Oil identifies the universities with graduates in the majors they seek, say, electrical engineers. An Edjali company representative completes an online job vacancy announcement, which zips over the Internet to the universities with electrical engineers.

These universities electronically respond with student resumes that meet the recruiting requirements.

Edjali Oil screens the applicant pool and selects its top electrical engineering candidates. Three may be at the University of Kentucky, one at the University of Maryland, two at the University of Tennessee and one at the University of Georgia. Rather than conducting on-site visits at each of these campuses, Edjali Oil contacts SEACnet's videoconferencing co-ordinator and sets up dates and times to interview all the top candidates.

If Edjali Oil has an internal videoconferencing system, the interviews will be conducted from its home base; if not, an Edjali recruiter travels to the nearest SEACnet videoconferencing site (let's say the University of Kentucky) to conduct the interviews with candidates at all the selected universities.

The big yet-to-be-resolved issue of this and other new electronic technology is who will pay. Some schools make participation in electronic job hunting mandatory or include it in the cost of scholarship; other institutions leave choice and payment up to each student.

Instead of familiar "face time," the new interviewing technology is unfamiliar "cyberspace time." Interviewing mannerisms need reevaluation; for instance, pausing and looking out the window before answering an interview question is considered thoughtful in person, but may look spacey on screen.

Videoconferencing is not expected to totally replace face-to-face interviewing even among its most enthusiastic users. In some situations, recruiters will use the videoconferencing as an initial screening tool to weed out all but the most promising candidates who will be interviewed in person, either on campus or at the company's offices.

College Electronic Resume Books

The electronic resume book is an example of what colleges and universities are doing to promote employability prospects for graduates. The New Jersey Career Center Network is compiling graduates' resumes into a scannable database for employers. says Richard L. White, director of career services at Rutgers University in New Brunswick.

A related database offers employers the opportunity to list job openings for students and alumni.

In addition to Rutgers, institutions participating when the consortium began in 1995 include Monmouth University, Fairleigh Dickinson University in Madison, Rider University, Ramapo College, and Trenton State College.

JOB DESCRIPTIONS HELP SHOW YOU HAVE WHAT THEY WANT

Any time you apply for a job, you're ahead of the pack when you know exactly the requirements of the position. This knowledge enables you to show how your qualifications are a good fit. If you can get a copy of the real job description from the advertising employer's human resource department, so much the better. Often, the real thing won't be available, so the next best thing is to visualize the duties and skills involved in the job.

On a sheet of paper, use the left side to write down what you think the job requires. On the right side, write down how you stack up. This comparison is immeasurably helpful in responding to a recruitment ad and for polishing your performance during the job interview. As an old saying goes, "You'll be loaded for bear."

Job Scribe

How it benefits you: Looking at job descriptions helps you sell yourself because it shows you know the tasks, lingo, and nature of the work.

This personal software for PCs enables you, the job seeker, to review accurate job descriptions. Job Scribe, Version 2.0 includes some 3,000 job descriptions. The program reportedly was developed using authentic job descriptions at all levels in actual organizations.

By using Job Scribe's data, you aren't trying to put one over on employers. You're not trying to come up with a phony resume with a rote listing of skills and experience that merely tells the employer what the employer wants to hear. You are, however, getting clues to appropriate language and terms to interpret your educational qualifications or work history.

Job Scribe, a reference tool rather than a home-use database, may be found at the reference desk of a large library, at school district offices, at city and county government complexes, and at college career centers.

JOB DESCRIPTIONS HELP SHOW YOU CAN DO WHAT THEY WANT

A refinement to the concept of using job descriptions to show you're a good match for the job has occurred since the passage of the Americans with Disabilities Act, now commonly known as ADA.

The passage of the ADA has swung open a big employment door long closed to many persons with disabilities. If you fit into this category, the next few paragraphs will be of substantial interest.

For the first time in history, job opportunities are available to the 70 percent of individuals with disabilities who are jobless—and don't want to be. Interviewers can no longer ask whether you have a disability, only whether you are able to perform the *essential functions of the position with or without reasonable accommodation.*

Despite ADA protection, the job world remains a jungle for the unwary who may—to their detriment—*inappropriately* blurt out a disability at the employment interview, or even on their resumes. Guard against that error by becoming informed on wise ways to use your new rights.

In this connection, here's an extra tip beyond reading job descriptions with an ADA twist. Buy or consult an outstanding book, *Job Strategies for People with Disabilities,* by Melanie Astaire Witt (Peterson's Guides, 1992). It is the first published effort to combine state-of-the-art career decision-making and employment-search techniques with the special interests of persons with disabilities. Quite simply, we think it's the single best career guide ever written for this readership.

The ADA will completely change the way American employers staff—exactly how, remains to be seen. Experts disagree about whether there will be an explosion of litigation.

Job descriptions are becoming more important: every word is being weighed against the ADA requirements. The ADA provides incentives for employers to plan ahead by creating written job descriptions before advertising or interviewing for positions.

A number of compliance tools are available to employers to help them cope with this rather complex law. As a job seeker, you will want to be aware of the lengths to which employers may go to ensure that all Americans—with or without disabilities—who want to work get an equal shot.

The following example of "ADA-safe" software is written to benefit employers who don't want to run afoul of the law. To discover the essential functions of a position—to help you know whether you can do the job with a reasonable accommodation—it's useful to step into the employer's shoes.

Where can you, the job seeker with a disability, screen the software? A straightforward call to the human resource department of a large company may get you an invitation. Ask whether the company has a diversity manager.

Here's another idea: Try a nearby "independent living center," which can be referred to you by the National Council on Independent Living, Troy Atrium, 4th Street and Broadway, Troy, NY 12180; Telephone (518) 274-1979 or (518) 274-0701. Names of centers vary. An example: The Access Center of San Diego, Inc.

If your local independent living center does not have an ADA-job-description database, its staff, being familiar with community resources for people with disabilities, may be able to suggest where else you might try.

Descriptions Now!

How it benefits you: If you have a disability, this job description program with ADA content can be used to determine whether you can do the work and how to position yourself in talking to employers.

This PC-based software program custom-writes complete job descriptions for the employer, in addition to facilitating every phase of employment to help comply with the ADA.

This program is for managers and employers who have little experience in writing job descriptions.

Descriptions Now! is available from KnowledgePoint, 1129 Industrial Avenue, Petaluma, CA 94952; Telephone (800) 727-1133. The program sells for less than $70.

In addition to the two above examples, a number of the applicant tracking systems we discussed in Chapter 3 offer tools within their programming to assist the employer in ADA compliance.

ADA protects individuals with physical or mental impairments, including those people who wish to return to work after such catastrophic events as a heart attack or cancer treatment.

By official count, nearly one in five adults in this country has a disability. Maybe you're that one. If not, you probably know someone who is eligible to be protected by ADA. It's useful to know that employers, often through electronic assistance, are making an effort to meet the federal mandate to level the playing field.

SOFTWARE JOB SEARCH TOOLS

Computers were designed to ease the routine stress in our lives, allowing us to concentrate on more productive efforts.

Record keeping in a job search can be a killer, but it's one of those VIDs—Very Important Details. Now you can handle much, if not all, of it with computer software.

Sharkware Professional

How it benefits you: This career management program brings new meaning to "It's whom you know that counts." Sharkware is a superior total contact and activity management system for PCs. With this product, it's easy to stay in touch with your network of contacts that means so much to your lifetime success.

One of the newest software programs on the market includes advice and techniques from Harvey Mackay, top-ranked motivational speaker and author of *Swim with the Sharks Without Being Eaten Alive* and *Sharkproof.*

Sharkware, which requires a 386 (or higher) IBM-compatible PC, Windows 3.1, and a VGA color monitor (equipment many people have today), manages information important to your immediate job search as well as to your long-term career success.

It stars the Mackay 66, a 66-question profile on the care and feeding of contacts, a profile recognized as one of the author's most effective methodologies.

The easy-to-use computerized version of the Mackay 66 covers seven categories of information for each contact: (1) education, (2) family, (3) business background, (4) special interests, (5) life-style, (6) the user's relationship with the contact, and (7) traditional address book entries.

Additionally, Sharkware has features such as unlimited addresses and space for comments. It comes with a fully integrated appointment calendar, a "to-do" list space, and a telephone call manager.

Sharkware is modestly priced. Find it in software stores, or order it through CogniTech Corporation, P.O. Box 500129, Atlanta, GA 31150; Telephone (800) 947-5075.

WHEN THE COMPUTER IS YOUR COUNSELOR

Are you considering heading off in a new direction in your life, either because you want to or because you have to?

If so, you can get help recycling yourself with one of the new software packages designed to help you make career decisions. You'll want help with personal assessment in such areas as general interests, academic interests, work-related interests, general abilities, aptitudes, values, work environment preferences, education level, and choice of working with people, data, or things.

Remember, view these packages as the first step in your new direction, not the final decision. You'll need to supplement them with lots of first-hand research. Here are tools that can help.

Career Design

How it benefits you: This product is the software version of the high-end career counseling method developed by the late John Crystal and his surviving partner, Nella Barkley. The live seminar format lasts a week and costs several thousand dollars.

Career Design is aimed at anyone who is considering a career change. The program is divided into more than 50 modules. Through a series of questions, they lead the career changer to such key realizations as: "Who am I?" "What do I really want?" "How do I get what I really want?"

Through interaction with the computer, you discover your interests and skills, how to set goals, how to negotiate, and how to cope with many other challenges you must master to change careers.

Career Design is attractive not only for its simplicity, comprehensiveness, and excellent value, but also for its in-depth expertise.

Career Design works on any IBM-compatible PC and is available for under $100 from Crystal-Barkley Corp., 23rd Floor, 152 Madison Avenue, New York, NY 10016; (212) 889-8500

Jumpstart Your Job Skills

How it benefits you: The most important thing you have to sell an employer is your skills. Beyond the obvious core abilities, many people have trouble illuminating their entire skillsets. This computer software product responds to a long-standing need in job search—figuring out exactly what you have to sell in the job market.

Written by well-known career development leaders Dave Swanson, Dick Knowdell and Jim Hurd, *Jumpstart Your Job Skills* software is an important self-marketing research tool. In fact, it is wonderful—the best skills analyzer we've seen! Using bright and appealing graphics—plus sound if you have a sound card in your computer—Jumpstart helps you inventory the skills you have, but may be failing to spotlight, into a powerful presentation package that will cause employers to sit up and notice.

Specifically, Jumpstart software shows how to identify and prioritize skills and use them to increase your value on compelling and highly targeted resumes. The program makes it easy to customize resumes—matching job requirements with your qualifications—by clicking on the "Enter New Idea" icon. Jumpstart is available for both PCs (Windows) and Macs.

Jumpstart retails for $70; order from Up Software, 7222 Lombard Street, #204, San Francisco, CA 94133; Telephone: (800) 959-8208.

Shareware: "Looking for Work"

How it benefits you: The shareware concept lets you try a software program on the cheap, usually for a few dollars. If it works for you, you're honor-bound to pay the full price of the program. It's a bargain.

Shareware is like a self-published book—it's software that has been written by an electronic author who hasn't hit prime time as yet. More often than not, the quality of shareware is top-notch. It usually costs less than $4 or $5 to try.

It's called "shareware" because the author is "sharing" his or her program with you. The publisher is trusting you, hoping that if you can use it, you'll pay what the software is really worth. The requested full payment for shareware usually runs between $5 and $100.

Virtually any vendor offering shareware will have at least one or two job search software programs. They are like new television sets—all of them will work, but you'll like the picture on some better than on others.

One we like very much, which comes highly recommended from out-placement firms that have used it extensively, is: Looking for Work: An Interactive Guide to Marketing Yourself.

Looking for Work is an interactive guide designed for professionals and managers who seek to change jobs or who have been laid-off or fired. Many have never been through a job search and need substantial help on even the most basic tasks and activities. Others will gain from a systematic approach.

The instructional software takes you step-by-step through eight units of instruction, augmented by dozens of worksheets to guide your job search.

The theme is that a job search is a marketing campaign and requires planning, analysis, targeted markets, and commitment to a schedule of tasks and activities. The program features a multi-track; that is, it directs you to the track best able to help you based on your age, income, current employment status, motivating factors, willingness to relocate, and level in the organization. This is a great feature because it goes straight to your bottom line.

When you complete the program, you will have a list of potential employers, a core resume, and marketing letters, and you will be prepared for interviews.

Specifically, the Looking for Work program will:

1. Help you develop a personalized plan, including a timetable and specific activities.
2. Help analyze your financial resources.
3. Give guidelines on preparing lists of target companies and other sources.
4. Provide forms, information, and guidance in preparing a detailed employment history.
5. Teach you how to prepare industry-specific resumes and marketing letters.

6. Structure week-by-week lists of tasks and activities, and identify milestones you can use to gauge your progress.

7. Identify online job listing and resume banks that may be appropriate for your experience and show why traditional resumes are unlikely to be effective.

8. Prepare you for what to expect in job interviews, including standard questions that may come your way.

You can obtain an examination copy of Looking for Work for less than $10. If you think it helps you, the full licensing fee for the new edition is $29. Licensing for institutional use is priced professionally; query the publisher.

Looking for Work is written and published by InterDigital, Inc., 742 Rt. 625, Hampton, NJ 08827; Telephone (908) 735-8979. It works on any IBM-compatible PC.

Shareware software is like a book; it cannot be read by two different persons at the same time. The software can be used by any number of people as long as it stays available for use at one location at a time.

Your new job may be mere keystrokes away.

TOPJobs

A database launched in late 1995, TOPjobs is described by creators Dynamic Information System and eXchange, Inc. (DISX) as one-stop shopping for the best jobs open to managers, professionals and technical specialists.

Each of the some 100,000 job listings is said to be current; the listings not obtained directly from employers are purged after 30 days, according to Eric E. Marchant, chief executive officer of DISX.

Job openings are obtained from employers, industry trade journals, job hotlines, newspapers, the Internet, and other publicly available sources.

The delivery system is a CD-ROM based package. It includes software for creating cover letters, mailing labels and managing contacts. The system will be available on the Internet before 1996.

Currently, you can reach in for jobs in one of three ways.

- The least expensive—and often free—method is to use TOPjobs at a library, outplacement service, or college career service office. (In these settings, the TOPjobs may be distributed by Ameritech Library Services' Visa service.)

- Alternatively, you can dial a toll-free 800 telephone number (not available at press time) and you will pay according to the number of the job matches made. That is, you specify the criteria of the job you want, and then a job search consultant searches the TOPjobs database and issues a report that matches current job listings with your specifications.
- The third way now available is to order an individual subscription for three-month periods at a cost of $150. You'll receive your own copy of the CD-ROM database each month.

More information is available from DISX, 275 East Center Street, Provo, Utah 84606; telephone (801) 377-3479.

TOOLS FOR HELP IN WRITING RESUMES

Using software to produce your resume has two big advantages over old-style typewriting and printing:

1. Greater flexibility to tailor the document to varying objectives.
2. Low-cost production of quality resumes.

You don't really need a computer program to punch out quality resumes, but it may be the path of least resistance for a neophyte resume writer.

A visit to your computer software store will show a wide variety of choice. Here are a few examples to illustrate the genre.

The Resume Kit (Spinnaker Software)

Re$ume! (North American InfoNet)

ResumeMaker (Individual Software, Inc., San Carlos, California)

Ready to Go Resumes (Yana Parker, Ten Speed Press, Berkeley, California)

WinWay Resume (WinWay Corporation, Sacramento, California)

USE E-MAIL TO CONTACT EMPLOYERS

E-mail is flashing fast: It is sent and received within seconds—or minutes, at most. All you need is access to an online information service, an e-mail program, and the e-mail address of the person with whom you wish to communicate.

Rising career stars, particularly those with a technical bent, are beginning to send unsolicited resumes and cover letters by e-mail to selected employers. E-mail can be limited to a single recipient or it can reach out and touch hundreds of employers.

At this writing, there are two sticking points with using e-mail for targeted job search.

The first is that e-mail is not very secure. Once you send an e-mail message into the ether, you have no control over its privacy. Online correspondence easily can be saved, called up at a later date, and sent out to a large number of people.

The second problem with e-mail in the job search is that finding e-mail addresses can be difficult. E-mail addresses are beginning to appear on business cards and in some e-mail directories, but comprehensive online directory assistance isn't available yet, as it is for telephone numbers. You can, of course, call the target executive's office and ask for the e-mail address.

MEET THE ELECTRONIC CAREER CENTER

It was bound to happen: a one-stop computer resource for career decision making. This concept is broader than Career Design, Peterson's Career Planning Service, and the shareware products described earlier in this chapter.

Once out of school, career choosers and career risers needed someplace to turn for vocational planning assistance. Of life's decisions, zeroing in on the right career field is one of the most tortuous for many people.

Here's a brief look at a prototype career guidance service.

Dr. Job

How it benefits you: Ask questions and get answers about career matters that puzzle you.

This is a GEnie online careers advice column where subscribers can ask questions. Topics covered range from corporate politics to career decisions. Dr. Job answers as many questions as possible. Some of the questions may be used for future Dr. Job online columns. Information is kept confidential upon request, and names are not used.

To access, contact GEnie, 401 North Washington Boulevard, Rockville, MD 20850; Telephone (800) 638-9636.

ENTREPRENEURSHIP: HIRING YOURSELF

Are you the sort of person who wants to break away from the world of wages and work for yourself? Perhaps you want to start your own small business. Perhaps you just want to pad the way for a more comfortable retirement by putting your hours away from your regular job into a part-time business that will earn extra cash.

Whatever your motive, you'll need all the information you can lay hands on, from software programs that write a business plan to a way to stay in touch with people who can help you nourish your fledgling business.

Among the resources you should check are those that find businesses to buy, locate people with special skills, or put you in touch with others who share your problems.

Business Resource Directory

How it benefits you: This is like an "electronic yellow pages" plus an electronic reference library plus an electronic personnel service—all rolled into one.

A searchable online database, Business Resource Directory is published and maintained by the National Small Businesses Network. It is available on GEnie's online information service. The Business Resource Directory is a good marketing tool for businesses, as well as individuals looking for work.

It's a way for individuals and businesses to locate other small businesses, home workers (people who want to work at home but not start their own business), job seekers, products, services, suppliers, and government offices that offer help to little-guy businesses.

The Business Resource Directory lists trade magazines, associations, government agencies, wholesalers, distributors, service bureaus, and software programs.

To subscribe, contact GEnie, 401 North Washington Boulevard, Rockville, MD 20850; Telephone (800) 638-9636.

Home Office/Small Business RoundTable

How it benefits you: This special-interest group service allows you to talk to others anywhere in the nation who may have problems similar to yours—and learn about their solutions. You're among friends here.

An online resource on GEnie, the Home Office/Small Business RoundTable is designed to meet the informational and networking needs of owners of micro- and home-based businesses or those who want to start a business.

The Home Office/Small Business RoundTable offers three categories of information about starting and operating a small or home-based business:

1. *The Bulletin Boards*—part of the GEnie basic online service. This is the main activity center where subscribers introduce themselves, write comments or ask questions about business, and "talk" to each other—with the help of their computer keyboards, of course. Most questions left in the Bulletin Boards are answered within 24 to 48 hours by either Home Office/Small Business RoundTable staff or members.

2. *Electronic Reference Libraries*—thousands of files, including how-to information and shareware (low-cost software) and freeware (free software) programs for businesses.

3. *Real Time Conference Rooms*—GEnie's version of computerized conferencing. Conferencing is a many-to-many medium, not a one-to-one form of communication. Everybody gets in on the act. Your messages are available for everyone in the conference to read and respond to, and you can react to the reactions. Conferencing is somewhat like a combination of a call-in radio talk show and a conference telephone call, only it takes place on the computer.

Contact GEnie, 401 North Washington Boulevard, Rockville, MD 20850; Telephone (800) 638-9636.

YOUR CREDENTIALS: SHOW AND TELL

A resume that speaks and moves, as well as reports in print? That's the premise of *multimedia resumes* that contain photographs, video, and sound components along with text. As one observer describes this type of resume, it's "Your credentials plus a song and dance."

Is it really a good idea to add sound and graphics to your resume? Well, maybe yes, if you're a creative person trying to show your stuff in entertainment, educational instruction, training, advertising or the graphic or performing arts. Another category of professionals who may find multimedia resumes useful are engineers scientists showing schematics of their work.

The problem is, how can you be sure the receiver of your resume will take the trouble to watch it? Today most screeners are trying to save time weeding out inappropriate applicants—they don't have the extra minutes it takes, as a rule, to watch or listen to your performance.

The other problem with multimedia resumes relates to equal opportunity concerns. Employers don't go out of their way to court legal liability. Concerned about challenges of discriminatory hiring, employers generally prefer not to receive pictures of applicants with resumes.

Moreover, the time-honored concerns remain. A photo or video of you subconsciously may remind the interviewer of a disliked person, while in person the physical similarity vanishes.

Unless there's a good reason to present yourself via a multimedia resume, stick with paper or electronic text versions.

TRACKING YOUR CAREER AFTER YOU'RE HIRED

Once you've settled on your job and are off on a new career adventure, don't think for a minute that the new employment rules and tools are out of your life.

The applicant tracking systems described in Chapter 3, in effect, are used to do employee tracking after the hire.

From your rising-star viewpoint, post-hire employee tracking systems have two things going for them: (1) job posting and (2) internal recruitment.

In job posting, job vacancies are up for everyone to see. In manual systems, a notice is simply posted on a company bulletin board. When an electronic tracking system is in place, you fire up your computer and search the job openings, applying for those you want and think you can get.

In internal recruitment, however, the job may or may not be posted. Your resume—with all its keywords intact—is in the company database, just waiting to be called up. A human resource specialist fires up the company computer and searches for a match. With the new technology available, most companies using tracking systems will perform an internal search of current employees before going outside to fill a job.

When you upgrade your credentials with additional education, find out from your company's human resource department how you go about adding that information to your employee file.

Beyond job posting and internal recruitment possibilities, you'll be glad to know that, with the help of your new employer's human resource department, you can probably find in a flash the key information about your employment. Many employee tracking systems continue to enter facts into your records once you're on board.

Aside from the obvious information—your name, address, physical description, educational background, and work experience previous to your employment (in other words, your resume)—employee tracking systems keep tabs on virtually all employment-related matters. These include your job title, salary history, benefits, equal employment opportunity classification, division or department assignment, performance evaluations, work review dates, next scheduled performance evaluation, and next salary review.

The employee tracking system records the amount of vacation you've earned. It tallies overtime or comp time records, and notes your insurance expiration date and how many insurance premium payments have been made and by whom. The software records your income tax and social security data, plus any payroll withholding information.

Some programs have complete background information on your family, your dependents and their dates of birth, and emergency contacts—information necessary for all sorts of insurance and emergency purposes.

Many employee tracking systems keep records of all officially required safety and injury data. Companies that offer retirement programs maintain complete records with the magic of employee tracking systems.

ON THE HORIZON

If some of the technological whistles and buzzers we've described thus far have your mind spinning, brace yourself for the pathway into the next century. As we become increasingly aware of the role electronics plays in our work—the very foundation of our lives—we will want to pay more attention to the changing tools and the changing rules.

In our visions of tomorrow's workplace, the most startling new tool we see is digitized information dressed up in a wardrobe of new applications.

Trend followers know that information is going digital. Text, sound, and pictures all are being translated into those same zeros and ones that computers read. High-definition television (HDTV), ready to make its debut, is but one example of digital technology.

Bill Gates, the young and dazzling CEO of Microsoft, calls the technotrend "the new digital world order."

The larger question is which future will electronics create? A utopia filled with job searches easier all around on both seekers and hirers? Or a world where people warehouse themselves with make-work, waiting for computers to find them a position of intrinsic value?

In the immediate future, it seems fairly sure that electronic trends begun yesterday will continue tomorrow—primarily because they are cost-effective. Videoconferencing, for instance, is likely to grow fairly rapidly, to save the costs of flyback interviews.

As the electronic dimension augments other forms of job search, in our opinion, millions of people will benefit.

AND, FINALLY . . .

We are sure the job search revolution we've reported in this book—and in our companion guides, *Electronic Resume Revolution* and *Hook Up, Get Hired!*—has begun and is picking up steam today. Gathering the information about what's happening has made believers of us.

As new tools continue to appear, here are two rules to remember:

1. Technology is moving job search to the people, not people to the job search.
2. Ignore the job search revolution at your own risk. It's the change of the century. Start now to learn the new ropes—and gain The Big Edge.

Computer Terms Made Simple

analog   Numerical values represented by physical variables such as voltage, current. Analog devices are characterized by dials and sliding mechanisms. See also *digital.*

application software   Computer programming allowing the user to perform specific tasks such as word processing or accounting.

ASCII   A universal code most desktop computers understand. Shorthand for American Standard Code for Information Interchange, and pronounced "askee." It's not easy reading.

audio   Sounds for the human ear used by multimedia systems.

baud   A measurement of speed at which information is transferred over a modem from one computer to another. Similar to BPS (bits per second), but not exactly the same. Computer buffs say the term "baud" is outdated and BPS is more accurate. But, right or wrong, you'll see the terms used interchangeably. The workhorse BPS speed today is 2400. Many people have 9600 BPS modems, or 14,400 BPS modems. The higher the number, the faster the information zips along telephone lines and the cheaper your telephone bill (if you're paying).

BBS   Bulletin board system—a computer that has been connected to a telephone line through a modem. Computer users can then phone a specific BBS and swap information, computer files, programs, or fellowship. An electronic meeting place where users with common interests exchange information.

binary system   A code that translates all letters and numbers into combinations of ones and zeroes. As a job seeker, you really don't care, but the term is so common you should know what it means.

bit   The smallest unit of computer information—either a one or a zero.

BPS   Bits per second. See *baud.*

byte   The amount of space it takes to store a single character on a disk—usually a chunk of four to eight bits, representing a single number, letter, or other character. The word "dog" takes three bytes of information.

CD   Compact disk—optically read disk. CDs can hold a ton of information. Machines read them.

CD-I   Compact disc-interactive—a compact disk format that provides audio, digital data, still graphics, and limited motion video. For a presentation, it's the works!

CD-ROM   Compact disk-read only memory—a way to permanently store mountains of data.

central processing unit   Called the CPU, it's the brain of the computer.

character   One letter, number, or figure.

chips   Very small squares or rectangles holding electronic circuits. Chips hold from a few dozen to several million electronic components, such as transistors and resistors. The terms *chip, integrated circuit,* and *microelectronic* all mean the same thing.

clone   A copy of an existing computer design.

compatible   A term used to describe computers capable of operating the same software.

computer literacy   A state of being fluent in computerese.

computer program   A very specific, very explicit, set of instructions given to a computer to perform a task or tasks.

computerese   A special language spoken by users, power users, hackers, and nerds. You can become old and gray before you become fluent in computerese. Words like "upload" and "digitize" are prime examples. Upload means to get the stuff up and out of your computer and into somebody else's computer. *Digitize* is described below.

DAT   Digital audio tape—a consumer recording and playback medium for high-quality audio.

data   Information.

database   A structured collection of related information. A common example is a computerized file of resumes that a computer can call up on command.

desktop publishing   The function of creating complex documents that integrate text, graphics, and different styles of type. Some job seekers who understand desktop graphics junk up their resumes trying to use all the available bells and whistles.

device   A general term for a piece of equipment attached to the computer. See *peripheral device.*

digital   The use of numbers. The word is derived from digit, or finger. Today, digital is synonymous with computer.

digitize   Convert information to binary codes—the ones and the zeros.

directory   A summary of the information contained in a computer or on a disk, as well as a map of how to locate that information; similar to a table of contents.

disk   A storage device within a computer, usually called the computer's "hard drive" or "hard disk," or a floppy disk that moves from computer to computer.

disk drive   Computer hardware; utilizes floppy disks, hard disks, or both.

disk operating system   Commonly known as DOS—a very basic software program allowing the computer to obey your commands as well as the commands of application software. MS-DOS and Windows are two well-known disk operating systems.

display   What you see on the computer screen (monitor).

document   A file such as a "text" produced by a word processing program.

dot matrix   A simple type of printer that utilizes pins to imprint tiny dots of ink onto paper. For resumes, if you use a dot matrix printer, make sure it's a 24-pin dot matrix to achieve near-letter quality.

dots per inch   Usually noted as DPI; refers to the quality of print or graphics, as measured by the density of individual dots of ink. The more DPI, the better the quality.

download   To receive information from another computer.

e-mail   Electronic mail automatically passed through computer networks and/or by modems over common-carrier lines. Beginning to be used for job-hunting letters.

facsimile   Commonly known as fax; a system used for the transmission of images of documents over telephone lines.

file   A collection of related computer information, usually organized in a directory.

font   A collection of letters and other characters used in printing type; all are the same typeface and the same size. `Courier 10 point,` **`Courier Bold 12 point`**, and *`Courier Italic 10 point`* are three separate fonts.

format   A command that tells the computer to create logical sectors on a disk, readying it to accept information. Or, when you format a document, such things as margins, spaces, and lengths of lines.

gigabyte   Approximately 1 billion bytes.

glitch   A problem, a malfunction.

hard disk   A storage medium that is a permanent part of the computer, stores large amounts of information, and accesses that information very rapidly.

hardware   In the world of computers, anything you can touch.

integrated circuit   Tiny pieces of silicon onto which electronic circuits are formed (see *chips*). Not to be confused with "silicon."

INTEL   The U.S. company that developed and produced the microprocessor that makes the PC possible. The term "386" or "486" comes from Intel 80386 or 80486 equipment.

interface   Computerized communication between peripheral devices— CPU to printer or CPU to mouse.

kilobyte   A total of 1,024 bytes.

kiosk   A stand-alone information delivery system often used for retail directories and other interactive information and sales presentations. Employment kiosks are beginning to appear; they present applicants with on-screen applications to fill out.

LAN   Local area network—a hooking together of two or more computers in one location.

laser printer   A printer that uses laser technology to print high-quality text and graphics. A laser-printed resume and cover letter is state-of-the-art.

letter quality   A term for print characters of a quality suitable for business correspondence and similar to that of a typewriter.

Macintosh   A brand name for one of Apple Computer's most popular graphics and text PCs.

megabyte   Approximately 1 million bytes—known as a "meg," or referred to in print as MB.

megahertz (MHz)   A measure of the speed or frequency at which the CPU operates, stated as millions of cycles per second.

memory   A computer's primary storage devices—the RAM, hard-drive, ROM, internal memory.

menu   A list of choices within a computer program; just what it says— dishes to be served up.

monitor   The television-like screen allowing the user to see what the computer is doing.

mouse   A pointing device used instead of a keyboard to give a computer rapid commands. Many people think it's easier to use a mouse than a keyboard.

multimedia   The delivery of information that combines different media—motion video, audio, still images, graphics, animation, text.

multimedia computing   Refers to the delivery of multimedia information through computers.

network   A system of hardware and software allowing one computer to work together with others, usually devoted to a common job or function. (See *LAN* or *WAN.*)

OCR   Optical character recognition, a software program loaded onto a PC. It works in conjunction with a scanner to read documents. OCR is how your bank uses a computer to read your checks.

offline   Not currently working. A condition of being functional but not operating.

online   Working great. Up and running. Electronically hooked up. A condition of being functional and operating.

operating system   Software that creates the environment in which the hardware, software, and operator interact—as in "disk operating system."

peripheral device   A device that attaches to the motherboard (CPU), enhancing the computer system's capabilities.

personal computer   A desktop-type computer likely to be used by an individual or small business.

power users   Extremely knowledgeable computer enthusiasts who eat, breathe, think, and sleep computing.

public domain   A term for any material—including software programs— that can be freely copied and used with no copyright infringements.

RAM   A commonly used computer term for random access memory—the working memory of the computer's system.

realtime   In computing, refers to an operating mode under which data are received and immediately processed. The results are returned instantaneously. It means "right now"—not later.

ROM   Read only memory—information permanently stored on microchips. It cannot be altered.

scanner   An input device that digitizes information. It's the machine equivalent of human eyes.

semiconductor   A term describing the electrical properties of elements such as silicon.

shareware   Similar to software in public domain, shareware is written by authors who allow users to try the product before buying it. Sometimes it's free and sometimes it costs a few dollars. If the author so requests, anyone using shareware is morally obligated to send the author a contribution.

software   Any set of instructions for computers. It commonly is issued on disks.

spreadsheet   Computer software designed to manipulate financial or statistical information, and, by performing complex mathematical calculations, to answer "What if . . . ?" questions.

systems software   Computer programs that give the computer sufficient instructions to get itself up and running and to maintain itself.

teleconference   A general term for a meeting not held in person. Usually refers to a multiparty telephone call, set up by a telephone company or private source, which enables more than two callers to participate in a conversation. The growing use of video allows participants at remote locations to see, hear, and participate in proceedings, or to share visual data (video conference).

UNIX   An operating system developed by AT&T, usually found on large computers.

upload   To send information from your computer to another computer.

user   Any person who directly "uses" (operates) a computer.

user-friendly   A term used to describe aspects of computing that require only a minimum of specialized knowledge—easily understood operation and instruction, as in "Almost anyone can do this."

VDT   Video display terminal—also known as a monitor.

VGA   Video graphics array. A super VGA means a color monitor.

WAN   Wide area network—as opposed to LAN, networking that connects computers over long distances, even continent-to-continent.

Windows   The trademark name of Microsoft, Inc., for its powerful, multitask, graphical software interface for DOS-based systems.

word processing   Typing with a computer.

WYSIWYG   "What you see is what you get"—a term used to describe what is on a computer screen accurately shows the image of a full page of a document. Pronounced "wizzy-wig," it's a good thing for you when your resume is WYSIWYG.

Index